High-Impact Worship Dramas

by John Duckworth

Vital
MINISTRY™
Loveland, Colorado

Dedication

To my fellow members of the Jericho Roadshow—Liz Duckworth, Bill Davis,

Tim and Karen Keller, and Lynn and Jeannette Conver—

whose willingness to try crazy things on church platforms has inspired me to do the same.

High-Impact Worship Dramas

Copyright © 1999 John Duckworth

Visit our Web site: www.grouppublishing.com

Credits
Editor: Dennis R. McLaughlin
Creative Development Editor: Dave Thornton
Chief Creative Officer: Joani Schultz
Copy Editor: Shirley Michaels
Art Director: Kari K. Monson
Cover Art Director: Jeff A. Storm
Cover Designer: Becky Hawley
Cover Photographer: Corbis Images
Computer Graphic Artist: Pat Miller
Production Manager: Peggy Naylor

Library of Congress Cataloging-in-Publication Data
Duckworth, John (John L.)
    High-impact worship dramas / by John Duckworth.
       p.   cm.
    ISBN 0-7644-2096-8 (alk. paper)
    1. Drama in public worship. 2. Christian drama, American.
I. Title.
BV289.D83 1999
246'.72--dc21
                                         98-56032
                                            CIP

10 9 8 7 6 5 4 3 2 1   08 07 06 05 04 03 02 01 00 99

Printed in the United States of America.

Contents

Introduction

Welcome to the Skit Book for *Every* Church!

Who could argue that using a meaningful skit in worship is a great idea? Not only will it add an element of active, visual learning to a worship service, but it also has the potential to strengthen a sermon in a very powerful way. A skit can brighten a worship service with humor and, at the same time, drive home a serious point. But only if it works!

Whether you've used lots of drama in your church or just a little, you may have discovered that some of your efforts have been less than satisfying. Maybe the scripts didn't make their points with power. Maybe the listeners couldn't hear your on-the-move actors because you didn't have wireless microphones. Or maybe some of your casts weren't composed of former drama majors and speech team captains. Welcome to the real world!

Fortunately, *High-Impact Worship Dramas* can help you successfully add drama to your worship—with less time and toil than you ever thought possible. The scripts in this book will help make stars out of your volunteer actors and a stage out of your worship area.

Real Fun, Real Truths—for Real People.

What do you want in a worship skit? Fun and excitement? You'll find it in the pages of this book—from parables to TV-show parodies. But maybe what you want is simply a solid Bible-based message. Then just keep turning the pages. You'll find the skits loaded with important topics— from prayer to friendship and from evangelism to Christ's return.

Even more than that, you'll get help to make each skit work for you. Every script in this book has been prepared with *real* churches in mind. But you're probably saying to yourself, "I don't have time to build an elaborate set." No problem—the sets are simple, and sometimes there's no set at all. If you have to use stationary microphones instead of the wireless type—no problem, because each skit includes easy-to-follow instructions on how to do just that.

Best of all, *High-Impact Worship Dramas* will help your actors draw the most meaning from every line. Each script features at-a-glance symbols that will *instantly* show participants how to put the right feeling into each line. You'll also discover that the words to be spoken with emphasis have been printed in all capital letters. This will help beat the "monotone syndrome" and ensure that the listeners catch key concepts.

The added benefit of using the skits in this book is that you'll build confident actors. The skits have been designed to cut mistakes to a minimum. Whatever the actors' abilities, the messages can't miss. The final result is that every audience member will hear, understand—and remember.

You can use *High-Impact Worship Dramas* in your worship services, Sunday school classes, Bible studies, retreats, or whenever you want to make a point in a fresh, funny, memorable way. Each script includes related Bible passages and a list of related topics that will simplify sermons and lesson planning.

A great skit can be one of your most valuable tools—if it works! So here's your chance to get your message off the page—and into the hearts of your audience where it belongs.

Key to Expression Symbols

To help actors know at a glance how to say their lines, the dialogue in this book includes simple facial-expression symbols. Most performers will quickly grasp the emotions represented by the symbols.

Calm, Pleasant

Happy, Hopeful

Laughing

Relieved

Serious, Earnest

Smug, Boastful, Condescending

Shy, Innocent

Nervous, Worried

Scared

Surprised, Shocked

Screaming, Hysterical

Malicious, Sneaky

Disgusted

Irritated, Complaining

Sad, Depressed, Sorry

Puzzled, Unsure, Thinking

Sarcastic, Skeptical

Mumbling, Whispering

Bored, Disinterested

Slick, Phony

Sheepish, Embarrassed

Proud, Haughty

Crying

Excited

Sick, Disoriented, Tired

Emotionless

Crazy, Goofy

Angry

Pained, Strained

Hypnotized, Zombielike

Account Your Blessings

Topic: Thanksgiving

The Scene: A living room

The Simple Setup: Place a table, flanked by two chairs, center stage. There should be a messy pile of papers on the table. **Miss Wickersham** will need a laptop computer (functioning or not), a personal digital assistant, or something resembling either of these.

The Sound: If you're using stationary microphones, put one near an imaginary door on the set. Place one or two microphones on the table as well. Have a helper ready to provide the knocking sound at an offstage mike. (A wireless or lapel mike will free Carper to pace back and forth; or simply have him deliver his "pacing" lines at the mike near the door.)

Other Options: If you can find an old-fashioned mechanical adding machine, the kind that makes a loud "totaling" sound when you pull the handle, you may want to use it in place of the computer. Pulling the handle and its accompanying noise will punctuate the dialogue nicely. If it's an electrical machine, you'll need an outlet into which **Miss Wickersham** can plug it.

The Characters:
    Christopher Carper, nervous "thankspayer"
    Miss Wickersham, businesslike (but not harsh) agent of the Eternal Revenue Service

*(As the skit begins, **Carper** nervously paces back and forth, often consulting his watch.)*

Carper: Where IS that guy? They're gonna nail me this time for SURE, I just KNOW it. *(Pauses.)* What am I TALKING about? I haven't done anything WRONG…HAVE I? It's just that I've never been…AUDITED before! *(He goes to the table and sorts papers.)* Boy, I hope HE'S IMPRESSED WITH these RECORDS! It took me TWO WHOLE HOURS to get 'em together…

*(**Wickersham** enters. She halts at the edge of the stage and knocks on an imaginary door. Sound of knocking.)*

Carper: AAUUGGH! *(The papers he's been sorting go all over the place; he tries in vain to gather them up. Finally he straightens up and answers the door.)*

Wickersham: Mr. Christopher CARPER?

Carper: NO! UH, YES, I mean, I didn't expect a…

Wickersham: I'm Miss WICKERSHAM from the E.R.S.

Carper: The E.R.S.?

Wickersham: The ETERNAL REVENUE SERVICE.

Carper: Oh, THAT E.R.S.!

Wickersham: The E.R.S. has asked me to conduct a routine AUDIT of your RECORDS.

Carper: *(In little squeaky voice)* OK.

(Wickersham comes in. Carper shuts imaginary door behind her. Wickersham goes to table and takes out a laptop computer.)

Carper: *(Pacing again)* I've…I've never been AUDITED before. I mean, I'm a GOOD guy. Well, I DID kick a DOG once. But it was a BIG dog! German SHEPHERD! PIT BULL! Uh…HALF German Shepherd, HALF pit bull—with TEETH the size of BOWLING PINS!

Wickersham: There's no need to be NERVOUS, Mr. Carper. The E.R.S. has chosen your case at RANDOM.

Carper: But I've heard all those STORIES…you know, about how you people SNOOP through private FILES, RUIN LIVES, DESTROY REPUTATIONS—not that there's any-thing WRONG with that!

Wickersham: You're thinking of the OTHER R.S., Mr. Carper. The ETERNAL Revenue Service has NEVER done that sort of thing. NEVER!

Carper: *(In little squeaky voice)* OK!

Wickersham: Now, after examining your THANKS RETURN…

Carper: My WHAT?

Wickersham: Your THANKS RETURN…that FORM you fill out every year, COUNTING your BLESSINGS.

Carper: You mean where I NAME THEM ONE BY ONE?

Wickersham: That's right. After EXAMINING your Thanks Return, we'd like to know WHY you re-turned so little THANKS this year.

Carper: Uh…DID I?

Wickersham: To BEGIN with, you failed to ITEMIZE your blessings.

Carper: Well, I used the SHORT form. It was a TERRIBLE year. REALLY!

Wickersham: That's what we're here to DETERMINE, Mr. Carper. WE have records TOO, you know.

Carper: *(In a little squeaky voice)* OK!

Wickersham: *(Firing up laptop)* Very well. I see that on JANUARY 24 of last year you received a substantial RAISE in SALARY.

Carper: Boy, I worked HARD for that one! I busted my—well, YOU know.

Wickersham: Yes, I KNOW. *(Punching buttons on computer)* FAILED to return THANKS.

Carper: But…

Wickersham: On MARCH 3 you recovered from a SERIOUS ILLNESS.

Carper: You can say THAT again. I thought I was gonna DIE! Good thing they've made all those ADVANCES in MEDICAL SCIENCE!

Wickersham: Uh-huh. *(Punching buttons on computer)* FAILED to return THANKS.

Carper: HEY!

Wickersham: Between June 19 and July 1 you CAMPED OUT in MONTANA. Our records show it didn't rain ONCE.

Carper: Oh, YEAH! Some GOOD LUCK, eh?

Wickersham: Right. *(Punching buttons)* FAILED to return THANKS.

Carper: Oh, MAN!

Wickersham: On SEPTEMBER 7 you SOLD A HOUSE for $5,000 MORE than you EXPECTED.

Carper: But that was just good BUSINESS sense!

Wickersham: I see. *(Punching buttons)* Mr. Carper, I'm afraid you FAILED to REPORT a SIGNIFICANT number of blessings last year.

Carper: *(Looking frantically through papers)* That can't BE! I've got RECEIPTS for EVERYTHING!

Wickersham: *(Punching buttons as **Carper** keeps searching his papers)* New SHOES…enjoyed watching a SUNSET…didn't slip on the ICE walking home from CHURCH…Reese's PEANUT BUTTER CUPS went on SALE…PHONE CALL from old FRIEND…got in a CAR ACCIDENT…

Carper: WAIT a minute! I'm supposed to be THANKFUL for a CAR ACCIDENT?

Wickersham: Mr. Carper, we have a MOTTO at the E.R.S.…."In ALL things, give THANKS."

Carper: But…

Wickersham: *(Punching buttons)* No serious INJURY in car accident…found HOUSE KEYS you'd lost…

Carper: WAIT! HOLD it! I don't keep records for such LITTLE things. You've got a list as long as my ARM, and we're still on JANUARY!

Wickersham: Well, Mr. Carper, it seems you owe a GREAT DEAL OF THANKS.

Carper: *(Squeaky voice)* OK! *(He clears his throat, then speaks normally but nervously.)* So, what's it going to BE? Do you throw me in JAIL? Take my HOUSE? Blow up my CAR?

Wickersham: No, Mr. Carper. *(Closes up computer.)* My work here is FINISHED.

Carper: Oh. You mean somebody ELSE is coming to TAKE ME AWAY?

Wickersham: No, no. You're FREE to GO.

Carper: FREE? HOW?

Wickersham: Giving thanks is VOLUNTARY, Mr. Carper. You have to WANT to do it. *(She gets ready to leave.)*

Carper: WANT to? Well, of COURSE I want to! *(Follows her to imaginary door, which she opens.)* HEY, I'll tell you what I'll DO. I'll make it all UP to you! I–I'll EAT A GREAT BIG DINNER! Yeah, THAT'S it! TURKEY and DRESSING, CRANBERRIES and SWEET POTATOES, PUMPKIN PIE and…

Wickersham: Exactly what would be the PURPOSE of eating all this food, Mr. Carper?

Carper: Why, to show how THANKFUL I am!

*(**Wickersham** looks at audience as if **Carper** is crazy.)*

Wickersham: Uh...THANKS...but NO thanks. *(She exits.)*

Carper: WELL! Talk about INGRATITUDE! I was even going to declare it...a NATIONAL HOLIDAY!

▶ **Related Scriptures:**
- Psalm 100
- 1 Thessalonians 5:16-18
- James 1:17

▶ **Related Topics:**
- Rejoicing despite trials
- God's goodness
- God's provision

Where Babies Come From

Topic: God the Creator

The Scene: A college lecture hall

The Simple Setup: Place a podium or pulpit center stage for **Professor**. Have him include a copy of the script in the notes he carries, which he can refer to as needed. **Student** should sit in the front row of the sanctuary. If possible, dress **Professor** in stereotypical academic garb—tweedy jacket with elbow patches, bow tie, and so on. He could "smoke" a pipe, too. **Student** should dress casually.

The Sound: You'll need a microphone at the podium and one in the front row where **Student** sits.

Other Options: If your **Professor** can do a passable impression of the late John Houseman's imperious Professor Kingsfield *(The Paper Chase)*, it will add an additional element to the skit. If not, stick with generic pomposity and condescension.

The Characters:
  Professor, pompous and condescending
  Female student, (Ms. Parker), earnest and nervous

*(As the skit begins, **Student** is in the front row of the sanctuary, sitting at a microphone. Enter **Professor** with a sheaf of notes. He puts his notes on the podium and addresses the audience as if it were his class.)*

Professor: WELCOME, class, to BIOLOGY 201! Today we will address a subject of GREAT IMPORTANCE. It is a subject that for SOME of you may be CONTROVERSIAL, even EMOTIONAL! But this is a BIOLOGY class, where we deal with EVERY issue in the CLEAR, COLD LIGHT of SCIENTIFIC FACT! *(Pauses.)* I'm talking, of course about the AGE-OLD QUESTION…"WHERE DO BABIES COME FROM?"

Student: *(Standing and raising hand)* Uh…PROFESSOR?

Professor: YES, Ms. Parker?

Student: I think MOST of us already KNOW the answer to that question.

Professor: Oh, DO you? TELL me, Ms. Parker, where DO babies come from?

Student: Uh…from PARENTS?

Professor: Ah! I see we have a CHILDRENIST among us!

Student: CH–CHILDRENIST? NO, NO! It's just that I was always TAUGHT…

Professor: You were ALWAYS TAUGHT, INDEED! That's why you've come to COLLEGE, Ms. Parker—to UNLEARN what you were always taught!

Student: Uh…YES, Sir. *(She sits.)*

Professor: I suspect that MANY in this group—like Ms. Parker—have been MISLED by SUPER-STITION, LEGENDS, and OLD WIVES' TALES regarding this question. And no WON-DER! Since the dawn of HISTORY, man has tried to imagine WHERE BABIES COME FROM. Every culture on the GLOBE has some kind of BIRTH MYTH in its earliest writings. For SOME reason, a common THREAD runs through all of them…a thread that has come to be known as CHILDRENISM. *(Pauses.)* As Ms. Parker has already INFORMED us, this PRIMITIVE NOTION holds that babies come from…*(makes quotation marks in air with fingers)* "PARENTS." In other words, babies are the *(makes more quotation marks in air)* "CHILDREN" or *(makes more quotation marks)* "OFFSPRING" of ADULTS. *(Pauses.)* This theory sounds SILLY to most of us today. But we must remember it was concocted by people who had never HEARD of DNA or DVD or even those AEROSOL CANS THAT SQUIRT CHEESE! *(Pauses.)* CHILDRENISTS believed in the idea of ADULTS who actually *(makes quotation marks)* "PRODUCED" the baby. How ABSURD! After all, who were these *(makes quotation marks)* "PARENT" beings, and how did THEY come to be?

Student: *(Standing and raising hand)* Uh…PROFESSOR?

Professor: YES, Ms. Parker?

Student: If—if Childrenism is so RIDICULOUS, why do some people BELIEVE it? *(She sits.)*

Professor: The answer is SIMPLE. They DESPERATELY WANT to believe! According to Chil-drenism *(makes quotation marks in air)*, "PARENTS" are wonderful beings who *(makes quotation marks in air)* "PRODUCE" babies as expressions of *(makes quotation marks in air)* "LOVE," then lovingly *(makes quotation marks in air)* "CARE FOR" and *(makes quotation marks in air)* "PROTECT" the babies. How COMFORTING! These PARENT beings, you see, are superior to babies in every WAY…STRONGER, TALLER, WISER, and more SELF-SUFFICIENT. *(Laughs.)* No WONDER the weak-minded prefer to believe in PARENTS! It makes the world seem a KINDER, GENTLER place! *(Pauses.)* And that's not ALL. Childrenism claims that babies are *(makes quotation marks)* "BROUGHT FORTH" in their parents' *(makes quotation marks)* "IMAGE." Thus, the Childrenist can feel IMPORTANT and ACCEPTED, believing he or she is much like his or her pre-existent, powerful *(makes quotation marks)* "FATHER" or *(makes quotation marks)* "MOTHER." PATHETIC, isn't it? *(Pauses.)* Very WELL. We can see that while primitive man thought PARENTS made BABIES, the exact OPPOSITE was true! BABIES invented the idea of PARENTS! Unable to explain in SCIENTIFIC terms the strange, new world in which they found themselves, BABIES banded together and came up with the concept of CHILDRENISM!

Student: *(Standing and raising hand)* Uh…PROFESSOR?

Professor: YES, Ms. Parker, what is it NOW?

Student: Has the theory of Childrenism been PROVEN wrong?

Professor: PROVEN, indeed! There is no NEED to prove it wrong! Not when courageous SCI-ENTISTS, hounded by backward CHILDRENISTS, have discovered the TRUE answer to the question that puzzled humanity for eons. *(Pauses.)* I am SPEAKING, of course, about the THEORY OF ELEVATION!

Student: *(Standing and raising hand)* Uh…PROFESSOR?

Professor: YES…MS.…PARKER?

Student: If ELEVATION is a THEORY, doesn't that mean it might still be DISPROVEN?

Professor: IMPOSSIBLE! Though it is still CALLED a theory, EVERY respectable scientist on EARTH knows it as absolute FACT! A handful of UNEDUCATED PERSONS still cling to CHILDRENISM, but the CIVILIZED WORLD has come around to the TRUTH!

Student: *(Standing and raising hand)* Professor?

Professor: MS. PARKER!

Student: According to the THEORY OF ELEVATION…where DO babies come from?

Professor: I thought you'd never ASK! *(Student sits.)* The Theory of Elevation is COMPLEX and difficult for the UNTRAINED to fully GRASP. But perhaps I can SUMMARIZE it. *(Pauses.)* Far, far away—no one knows exactly WHERE—a LARGE, LONG-LEGGED BIRD wraps an INFANT in a sling of CLOTH. This bird is called a STORK. That's S-T-O-R-K. The stork flies at a great ELEVATION—hence the theory's NAME—until it reaches a POPULATED AREA. There the stork chooses a HOUSE…totally at RAN-DOM…and drops the baby down the CHIMNEY into the occupant's waiting ARMS!

Student: *(Standing and raising hand)* Professor?

Professor: YES! YES, Ms. Parker!

Student: Where does the STORK get the baby?

Professor: IRRELEVANT! It is merely a matter of TIME before scientists answer that trivial question!

Student: *(Still standing, raising hand)* Professor?

Professor: WHAT? WHAT?

Student: What if you don't have a CHIMNEY?

Professor: In such RARE CASES, the baby comes from a LOW elevation. Those who want to *(makes quotation marks in air)* "HAVE A BABY" travel to an AGRICULTURAL area and locate a CABBAGE PATCH. After obtaining the farmer's PERMISSION, the searchers ENTER the cabbage patch and look under the LEAVES. When an infant is found at this LOW ELEVATION, the adults pick it UP and take it HOME with them! *(Pauses.)* The IMPORTANT thing to remember is that, regardless of the MEANS of arrival, babies just HAPPEN. Write that down! There is no *(makes quotation marks in air)* RHYME or *(makes quotation marks)* REASON to the process and certainly no *(makes quotation marks)* PARENT *(makes quotation marks)* BEING *(makes quotation marks)* WHO *(makes quotation marks)* creates *(makes quotation marks)* THE *(makes quotation marks.)* OFFSPRING! *(Pauses.)* Such SUPERSTITIONS as CHILDRENISM are best left where they BELONG…on the SCRAP HEAP of HISTORY!

Student: *(Standing and raising hand)* Uh…PROFESSOR?

Professor: YES, Ms. Parker! WHAT…IS…IT?

Student: Professor…Do YOU and your WIFE…have any BABIES?

Professor: Uh…well…er…I…um…NO.

Student: Why NOT?

Professor: *(After a pause)* I…DON'T…KNOW!!! *(Pauses.)* CLASS DISMISSED!

(He exits in a huff.)

▶ **Related Scriptures:**
- Genesis 1
- Deuteronomy 32:3-6
- Romans 1:18-25

▶ **Related Topics:**
- Reliability of the Bible
- Defending the faith
- Faith and reason
- Evolution

The Beetle With the Rolls-Royce Nose

Topic: Self-Worth

The Scene: A land far away

The Simple Setup: You'll need a partition, curtain, sheet, or scenery flat center stage, that will allow Beetle to be out of view during his transformation. Costumes may be as basic or as elaborate as you like, as long as they suggest the characters' identities as automobiles. Each "car" could wear a sweat shirt decorated with the appropriate auto maker's logo; or give each "car" a baseball cap with an auto maker's logo and two small aluminum-foil "headlights" on it. For **Beetle**'s Rolls-Royce nose, make a small (up to three inches square) radiator grille out of foil-covered cardboard, attach a rubber band, and have the actor wear it over his or her nose after the transformation takes place. For props, you'll need an old iron skillet, a hammer, and an electric drill. **Beetle** will need a handkerchief and a piece of paper.

The Sound: If you're using stationary microphones, place two or three of them across the stage at equal intervals. Plan your actors' movements so they're close to one of the mikes when they need to deliver their lines. You'll need an offstage mike for the **Mechanic**. For sound effects, use a real or recorded car horn when **Beetle** blows his nose. (An old-fashioned "aaoogah" horn will lend a comic touch.) During the transformation, try hammering on an old skillet and squeezing the trigger of an electric drill in short bursts.

Other Options: If you'd like more elaborate car costumes, try decorating large sheets of cardboard to look like the fronts and rears of the appropriate autos. Have actors wear these over their shoulders like sandwich boards. Or turn large cardboard cartons into car shapes, cutting holes through which the actors can stick their heads.

The Characters:
    Narrator, kind and gentle, as if telling a fairy tale
    Beetle, a childlike Volkswagen bug
    The Mechanic, unseen but compassionate
    Studebaker, old in mileage but young at heart
    Rolls-Royce, snobbish and quite British
    Ferrari, expansively Italian and proud of himself

*(The stage is empty as the **Narrator** speaks from offstage.)*

Narrator: FAR AWAY, in a land where CARS are MORE than mere STEEL and TRANSMISSION FLUID, there lived a BEETLE. *(**Beetle** enters, slowly "driving" in circles.)* He was a 1967 VOLKSWAGEN Beetle, with DENTS in his HOOD and GNATS on his WINDSHIELD. His TIRES were balding, and the SUN had baked the GLOSS from his paint.

(**Beetle** *stops, looking glum.*) Of ALL the cars in the LAND, BEETLE was the most MISERABLE.

Beetle: What a HOMELY thing I am! Even with a lot of MILEAGE, I don't seem to know where I'm going. I'm not GETTING anywhere...just driving around in circles. (*He takes out a handkerchief and blows his nose. Car horn sounds.*)

Narrator: He had TRIED the standard CURES...high-octane GAS, gold SPARK PLUGS, a sniff of ETHER in his CARBURETOR. He'd tried a VALVE job, a new STEREO, a hand-woven LITTER BAG, and even an AIR FRESHENER shaped like a PINE TREE. But nothing WORKED. Deep down he was STILL the same old BEETLE.

(**Ferrari** *enters.*)

Ferrari: HEY, ugly little car! What'sa you PROBLEM?

Beetle: Oh, it's YOU, Ferrari. I just can't seem to...

Ferrari: I know whatta you problem is! You not a FERRARI!

(**Ferrari** *exits, laughing.*)

Beetle: (*Sighing*) He's RIGHT. I'm just an ugly old BEETLE...and that's all I'll ever be. (*He blows his nose. Car horn sounds.*)

Narrator: ONE day, driving sadly down the HIGHWAY (**Beetle** *walks slowly across stage*), Beetle saw something that nearly made him CROSS the yellow line. (*Enter **Rolls-Royce**. **Beetle** stops and stares.*) It was a glistening ROLLS-ROYCE SILVER CLOUD, all dazzling CHROME and wire WHEELS. (**Beetle** *watches wistfully as the **Rolls** glides past.*)

Beetle: If only I were a ROLLS-ROYCE instead of a BEETLE...THEN I'd be happy. Everyone would look UP to me! (*He watches as the **Rolls** exits.*) Hey, WAIT a minute! I COULD have style! I COULD have class! (*He rummages in his pocket.*) I think I have just enough MONEY left in my GLOVE COMPARTMENT!

Narrator: Sputtering into HIGH GEAR, Beetle headed for the nearest ROLLS-ROYCE DEAL-ERSHIP. (*He goes behind the partition.*) And the TRANSFORMATION began.

(*Sounds of metal clanging, hammering, drilling.*)

Beetle: OW!

Narrator: ...Beetle said when they made the INCISION in his HOOD.

Beetle: OW!

Narrator: …He said again when the BILL was presented. *(Pauses.)* It took every penny Beetle HAD. But when he emerged from the BODY SHOP, he was SURE the ordeal had been WORTH it. *(**Beetle** comes out from behind the partition.)* There he WAS, the PROUD OWNER of a BRAND NEW ROLLS-ROYCE NOSE.

Beetle: WOW! It covers my old BEETLE nose PERFECTLY! I'm a NEW CAR! *(He runs around in a circle, making "vroom" noises.)* I've got to show the OTHERS. Won't THEY be impressed!

*(Enter **Ferrari** and **Rolls**. They stop short when they see **Beetle**.)*

Ferrari: Mama MIA! You got a NOSE JOB!

Rolls: Good GRIEF! What INCREDIBLY bad TASTE!

Ferrari: You looka like an EXPLOSION in a BUMPER factory!

Rolls: Give UP, you low-class CLATTERTRAP. You're not a Rolls NOW, and you never WILL be!

*(**Ferrari** and **Rolls** exit, looking smug. **Beetle** looks crestfallen.)*

Narrator: Beetle BLUSHED so hard that his ENGINE began to OVERHEAT. He chugged off the highway and SAT.

*(**Beetle** sits.)*

Beetle: I can SEE it now. NOTHING'S going to change. I'm STILL a homely old BEETLE, driving around in CIRCLES. I'll NEVER discover the MEANING OF TRANSPORTATION. *(He blows his nose. Car horn sounds.)* I can feel my BATTERY wearing down. Maybe this time I won't bother to RECHARGE it.

*(Enter **Studebaker**, who sees **Beetle** and sits nearby.)*

Studebaker: What's WRONG, Beetle?

Beetle: Who—who are YOU?

Studebaker: Oh, I'm just an old STUDEBAKER…1939, to be exact! YOU can call me STU.

Beetle: I don't GET it. How come you're so HAPPY? You're in worse shape than I am! But you look like—you seem to KNOW where you're GOING.

Studebaker: I DO! That's because I've got a PURPOSE. I got it from the MECHANIC!

Beetle: The MECHANIC? That wouldn't work for ME. I've BEEN to garages before.

Studebaker: You'll understand when you MEET the Mechanic. Go ahead…give him a TRY! He's about THREE MILES SOUTH, then turn RIGHT. BYE!

(Studebaker exits.)

Beetle: It'll NEVER work. *(He blows his nose. Car horn sounds.)* OH, well! I'll just stop by on my way to the JUNKYARD. *(He exits.)*

Narrator: Soon Beetle drove up to the BIG GARAGE. *(**Beetle** enters and looks around in awe, as if the whole sanctuary is the garage.)* He LOOKED AROUND in WONDER. Cars of ALL KINDS were there…some HUMBLER than the STUDEBAKER, some CLASSIER than the ROLLS-ROYCE. A FEW were being REPAIRED, but MOST seemed to be… GOING PLACES.

Mechanic: *(Offstage)* HELLO, Beetle.

Beetle: Who SAID that?

Mechanic: I did, Beetle.

Beetle: Are YOU…the MECHANIC?

Mechanic: That's RIGHT, Beetle. I've been EXPECTING you.

Beetle: I…met this STUDEBAKER…

Mechanic: I KNOW.

Beetle: Can—can you FIX me UP?

Mechanic: You KNOW I can, Beetle.

Beetle: The STUDEBAKER was RIGHT. There's something DIFFERENT about you. It's like you can SEE right through my ENGINE COVER…and you seem to CARE what's INSIDE.

Mechanic: Indeed I DO.

Beetle: But…how much will it COST?

Mechanic: EVERYTHING, Beetle. EVERYTHING.

Beetle: But I don't have any more MONEY. I spent it all on my ROLLS-ROYCE NOSE.

Mechanic: *(Chuckling)* I KNOW. But it's already PAID for, Beetle. All you have to do is SIGN OVER your TITLE and REGISTRATION to ME.

Beetle: WHAT? You mean you want to OWN me?

Mechanic: It's the only WAY.

Beetle: *(To himself)* WOW! This is like being TOTALED! *(He looks around.)* But all these OTHER cars…they've got places to go! *(Pauses, then to **Mechanic**)* OK. *(He gets a paper from his pocket.)* I—I hereby SURRENDER my TITLE and REGISTRATION. And my ROLLS-ROYCE NOSE. *(He takes off his Rolls nose and places it on the floor with the paper.)*

Mechanic: CONGRATULATIONS, Beetle!

Beetle: I—I feel NEWER than the day I rolled off the ASSEMBLY LINE! But…I don't UNDERSTAND. I'm still just a homely old 1967 BEETLE. How come I feel so DIFFERENT?

Mechanic: Because now you're MY homely old 1967 Beetle.

Beetle: AH!

Narrator: So THAT was the MEANING of TRANSPORTATION, Beetle thought…to be OWNED and OPERATED by the one who UNDERSTANDS you BEST. He listened CAREFULLY to the Mechanic's DIRECTIONS, then headed for the HIGHWAY, SMILING from BUMPER to BUMPER. *(**Beetle** exits.)*

▶ **Related Scriptures:**
- Psalm 40:1-8
- 2 Corinthians 5:17
- Galatians 6:12-15

▶ **Related Topics:**
- Becoming a Christian
- Being a new creation
- Finding meaning in life

The Boxing Match

Topic: What God Is Like

The Scene: A meeting hall

The Simple Setup: You'll need a podium at stage right, facing a row of three chairs that sit at stage left. All characters should wear "Sunday best" clothes. The box carried by **Nervous Man** should be constructed as follows: Cut an arm-sized hole in the base of a medium-sized cardboard carton. The actor carries the box with one hand through the hole and hidden in the box; with that hand he holds a small plastic baseball bat or cardboard tube. The lid of the box should be hinged so that, as needed, the bat or tube can pop out and hit him on the head. Other props include a child's lunch box, makeup compact with mirror, pocket-sized leather case and some papers (for **Emcee**), empty file cabinet (any size), hand truck or dolly, and a manila folder.

The Sound: If you're using stationary microphones, you'll need one at the podium, two in front of the chairs, and one about halfway down the sanctuary aisle (for **Man with File Cabinet**).

Other Options: The row of chairs could be replaced by a pew if desired.

The Characters:

> **Emcee**, a dapper man with the superficial smoothness of a TV game show host
> **Lady With Lunch Box**, bubbly and immature
> **Nervous Man**, carrying a cardboard box he seems deathly afraid of
> **Lady With Compact**, vain and self-absorbed
> **Man With File Cabinet**, a stern, older fellow who pushes a file cabinet on a hand truck

*(As the skit begins, there should be three people sitting in chairs across from a podium, as if waiting for a speaker to arrive. **Lady With Lunch Box** sits next to **Lady With Compact**, and **Nervous Man** sits next to them.)*

Lady With Lunch Box:		*(to **Lady With Compact**)* Oh, I LOVE these get-togethers! They're always so… INSPIRATIONAL!
Lady With Compact:		ABSOLUTELY! I just don't know what I'd do WITHOUT them. Or without HIM, of course! *(She holds up a makeup compact and points to it.)* I bring him with me wherever I GO, you know. He makes me feel so SAFE!
Lady With Lunch Box:		I know what you MEAN! *(She holds up a child's lunch box and leans her head against it.)* Just knowing he's THERE, all SNUG in this BOX, makes me so HAPPY to be a BOX HOLDER. When I think back to the OLD days, before I even KNEW you could PUT him in a box—why, I don't know how I managed to keep GOING!

*(**Emcee** enters, takes his place at podium, and shuffles some papers.)*

Lady With Compact: Oh, it's TIME! I can just feel my HEART beating a MILE a MINUTE!

Nervous Man: SSHH! *(He holds up a cardboard carton.)* You're DISTURBING him! He—he's very SENSITIVE!

Emcee: Good EVENING! SO nice to see you all HERE tonight…and so nice to see so many WONDERFUL BOXES! *(He pauses, his face growing somber.)* You KNOW, friends, we are SO blessed! SOME folks don't even KNOW about…HIM. They don't know you can TUCK him AWAY all SAFE and SNUG in your OWN PERSONAL CONTAINER. Let's TAKE a moment to THANK him, shall we?

*(**Lady With Lunch Box** holds up lunch box and gives it an affectionate pat. **Lady With Compact** holds up compact and gives it a little kiss. **Nervous Man** bows his head to his box. **Emcee** takes a leather case from his suit pocket and gives it a heartfelt wink.)*

Emcee: *(Huskily)* SUCH a blessing! *(He stuffs the case back into his pocket.)* HEY! Let's get this show on the ROAD! As you KNOW, one of the GREATEST things about getting together is SHARING with each other what's in our BOXES. So tonight I'm going to PICK a few of you at RANDOM to COME RIGHT UP and TELL us about the BOXES you've brought! Let's SEE…how about THIS lady? *(He points at **Lady With Lunch Box**.)* Come on UP!

*(**Lady With Lunch Box**, giggling, brings her lunch box to the podium and stands next to **Emcee**.)*

Lady With Lunch Box: Oh, I'm so EXCITED! I've always WANTED to get UP here and TELL everyone about…well, about YOU-KNOW-WHO!

Emcee: Here's your CHANCE! TELL us about the box YOU'VE brought.

Lady With Lunch Box: *(Holding up lunch box)* I keep him in a LUNCH BOX…to remind me of how he gives me EVERYTHING my heart DESIRES…like FOOD, for instance!

Emcee: Very GOOD! *(**Emcee**, **Lady With Compact**, and **Nervous Man** applaud.)* Does he give you anything BESIDES food?

Lady With Lunch Box: Oh, my, YES! He showers down CARS and BOATS and HOUSES and NICE CLOTHES and GOOD HEALTH and PERSONAL DIGITAL ASSISTANTS…

Emcee: I SEE! Sounds like you've got him in a BOX, all right!

Lady With Lunch Box: *(Giggling)* I sure DO! It's so COMFORTING to know he's THERE. He's done such a GOOD JOB that one of these days I may even TRADE IN this LUNCH BOX for a nice, roomy PICNIC BASKET!

Emcee: Now THAT'S a thoughtful idea! I'm sure he'll APPRECIATE it! Thanks SO much for SHARING.

*(The rest applaud as **Lady With Lunch Box** returns to her seat.)*

Emcee: *(Scanning the "audience")* Let's SEE…how about YOU, sir? *(He points at **Nervous Man**.)*

Nervous Man: M-ME?

Emcee: Yes, YOU! Come right UP, and tell us about YOUR box!

Nervous Man: W-well, all RIGHT. *(He comes toward the podium slowly, cradling a large cardboard carton, which he keeps glancing at anxiously.)*

Emcee: THAT'S it! Just come RIGHT UP here. No need to be FRIGHTENED.

Nervous Man: *(Watching his box as if it might explode any second)* Th-that's what YOU think!

Emcee: *(As **Nervous Man** reaches podium)* Now, THAT wasn't so bad, WAS it?

Nervous Man: N-not YET. B-but it could happen any TIME!

Emcee: WHAT could happen any time?

Nervous Man: H-he could get MAD! I never know when he might JUMP OUT and PUNISH me! When I least EXPECT it, he could decide to hit me with LIGHTNING BOLTS or a DISEASE.

Emcee: Why would he want to do THAT?

Nervous Man: Because he's like a POLICEMAN! He's always WATCHING me, waiting for me to DO something! *(He stares in horror at the box, talking faster and faster.)* I can just FEEL him getting ANGRY with me, and I always do something WRONG because I'm such a BAD PERSON, and he's OUT to GET me, and…and… *(His hand pops out of the box and bops him on the head repeatedly with the cardboard tube.)* AAUUGGHH! *(Still hitting himself over the head, he exits, preferably down the sanctuary aisle.)*

Emcee: *(After a pause)* WELL! As I always SAY, "To thine OWN BOX be TRUE"! Let's try ANOTHER box holder. *(Pointing at **Lady With Compact**)* How about YOU, ma'am?

Lady With Compact: *(Coming to the podium, she holds up a compact)* I just want to say that I've kept YOU-KNOW-WHO in this COMPACT for YEARS, and he would NEVER do anything to HARM or UPSET me. We're the BEST of FRIENDS! It's SUCH an encouragement to know that he wouldn't DARE IRRITATE or CONTRADICT me!

Emcee: I know that's been true in my OWN life! And why do you get along so WELL with him?

Lady With Compact: Because he's growing to be more and more like ME every DAY! Whenever I want to REMIND myself of what he's LIKE, I just glance in the MIRROR on this COMPACT …and there he IS! *(She opens compact and smiles adoringly at herself in the mirror.)*

Emcee: What a SWEET and PRECIOUS TRUTH! Thank you SO much! *(He takes out a handkerchief and dabs at his eyes as **Lady With Compact** returns to her seat.)* Let's have ANOTHER box holder come up and tell us…

Man With File Cabinet: *(Interrupts from the rear of the sanctuary)* STOP! I won't hear another WORD of this! Not another WORD! *(He comes up the aisle to the podium, pushing a file cabinet on a hand truck.)* I've listened to this HERESY long ENOUGH! All this nonsense about "YOU-KNOW-WHO" and putting him in BOXES. WHO do you people think you ARE?

Emcee: W-what do you MEAN?

Man With File Cabinet: You obviously have no CONCEPTION of what he's REALLY like! Lunch boxes, cartons, and compacts, INDEED! He's MUCH too big for ANY of those things!

Emcee: He IS?

Man With File Cabinet: Of COURSE! *(He pats his file cabinet.)* It's all right HERE, in my DOCTRINAL STATEMENT! *(He pulls a manila folder from the first drawer, clears his throat, and begins to read.)* I BELIEVE in the PRETRIBULATIONAL, PREDESTINATIONAL FOREKNOWLEDGE of the MULTI-DISPENSATIONAL SYSTEM of HERMENEUTICS! I BELIEVE in the SUBSTITUTIONARY IMMERSION of SANCTIFICATION, EDIFICATION, JUSTIFICATION, the OMNIPRESENT, OMNISCIENT, OMNIPOTENT, TRIUNE…

Emcee: YES! Why didn't we see this BEFORE? We've been so BLIND! SO blind!

Man With
File Cabinet: WELL! At least you ADMIT your error!

Emcee: Indeed we DO! But now we can CHANGE, thanks to YOU! *(He dabs his eyes with his handkerchief, then turns to the assembled box holders.)* My FRIENDS! Through THIS MAN'S shining EXAMPLE, at LAST we see how we may be FREE of our BOXES! *(**Lady With Lunch Box** and **Lady With Compact** look at each other with surprise and excitement.)* NO LONGER must we carry these CUMBERSOME CONTAINERS! As our visitor has SHOWN, we can leave YOU-KNOW-WHO at HOME…in a FILE CABINET!

Man With
File Cabinet: WHAT? But THAT'S not what I…

Emcee: Thank you SO much for sharing that LIFE-CHANGING INSIGHT! *(**Ladies** applaud. **Emcee** looks at his watch.)* My FRIENDS…once AGAIN our TIME has FLOWN. Thank you ALL for being part of this VERY special evening—and don't forget your BOXES!

*(**Emcee** gathers his papers from the podium and exits as **Man With File Cabinet** slowly walks back down the aisle, bewildered.)*

Man With
File Cabinet: What—what HAPPENED? *(He exits.)*

Lady With
Lunch Box: *(Standing)* I just LOVE these meetings! So INSPIRATIONAL, you know!

Lady With
Compact: *(Standing)* Isn't THAT the truth! *(She holds up compact.)* I think he'll look LOVELY in a FILE CABINET, don't YOU?

Lady With
Lunch Box: DIVINE! Absolutely DIVINE! *(They exit.)*

▶ **Related Scriptures:**
- Exodus 20:1-7
- Job 38
- Psalm 139

▶ **Related Topics:**
- Limiting God
- Putting God first
- The authority of Scripture

Casey at the Pulpit

Topic: Listening to God's Word

The Scene: A church sanctuary

The Simple Setup: You'll need a podium center stage. **Casey** will need a Bible and some notes.

The Sound: If you're using stationary microphones, put one at the podium, one or two offstage for **Readers**, and one at a front pew for **Church Member.** The "snoring sounds" (about two seconds of snoring each) can be provided by **Reader One** or by a recording.

Other Options: If you have sufficient lighting control, a total blackout at the end of the skit will enhance its impact.

The Characters:

    Pastor Casey, long-suffering but determined
    Reader One, precise and expressive
    Reader Two, like **Reader One**, but with a contrasting voice
    Church Member, loud and opinionated

*(As the skit begins, **Reader One** and **Reader Two** are at microphones offstage. **Church Member** sits at a microphone in a front pew. **Pastor Casey** stands at the side of the stage, holding a Bible, his head bowed.)*

Reader One: The OUTLOOK wasn't BRILLIANT at the MUDVILLE CHURCH that day;
Pastor CASEY, who was WORRIED, took one minute more to PRAY.
He KNEW that if his SERMON seemed to QUAVER, DRAG, or LURCH,
A SICKLY SILENCE soon would fall upon FIRST MUDVILLE CHURCH.

Reader Two: A RESTLESS FEW got up to go before his START. The REST
Sat in their pews like CORPSES, which was what they did the BEST.
They thought…

Church Member: *(Standing up)*
If only Casey were the ENTERTAINING type!
We'd even put up MONEY then; we'd like a little HYPE!

*(**Church Member** sits. **Casey** walks to the pulpit as **Reader One** speaks.)*

Reader One: For some EXCEEDED Casey, in their STYLE and in their DRESS,
Those TV PREACHERS, SINGING GROUPS, COMEDIANS, and the rest;
So upon that drowsy MULTITUDE grim MELANCHOLY sat,

For there seemed but little CHANCE of trading CASEY in for THAT.

Reader Two: *(As **Casey** mimes talking to the congregation)*
Then during the ANNOUNCEMENTS, to the wonderment of ALL,
The pastor told a JOKE and sent a GIGGLE through the hall!
*(**Casey** smiles and begins paging through the Bible as if finding a passage.)*
But when the dust had LIFTED and they saw what had OCCURRED,
He was taking out his BIBLE; he was going to teach the WORD!

Reader One: So from a hundred THROATS or more there rose a lusty YAWN;
It RUMBLED through the SANCTUARY, RATTLED on the LAWN;
It KNOCKED upon the STEEPLE and RECOILED upon the BEACH,
For CASEY, Pastor CASEY, would soon begin to PREACH.

Reader Two: There was HOPE in Casey's manner as he stepped into his PLACE;
There were NOTES on Casey's PULPIT and a SMILE on Casey's FACE.
And WHEN, responding to the YAWNS, he looked up at the CLOCK…
*(**Casey** looks toward rear of sanctuary.)*
Each STRANGER in the crowd could hear each little TICK and TOCK.

Reader One: Two hundred EYES were closing as he opened up the BOOK;
A hundred HEADS were nodding, planning Sunday ROASTS to COOK.
And while the CONGREGATION held their HYMNALS in their laps,
They settled down to take their LONG and SPIRITUAL NAPS.

Reader Two: *(As **Casey** mimes preaching)*
And now the opening BIBLE TRUTH came HURTLING through the air;
The members sat a-WATCHING it in haughty GRANDEUR there.
Close by the sleepy CHURCHMEN the truth unheeded SPED…

**Church
Member:** *(Standing up)*
That ain't our STYLE!…

*(**Church Member** sits.)*

Reader Two: …They mumbled.

Casey: *(Holding up index finger)*
Point ONE!…

Reader Two: …The pastor said.

Reader One: From the BENCHES, dark with PEOPLE, there went up a muffled SNORE,
Like the whirring of a BUZZ SAW on a stern and distant SHORE.

**Church
Member:** *(Standing)*
FIRE him! Fire the PREACHER!...*(Sits.)*

Reader One: ...Muttered someone in the pews;
But they'd fired so many ALREADY, there was no one left to CHOOSE.

Reader Two: *(As **Casey** loosens his collar and mimes preaching)*
With a smile of Christian CHARITY, poor Casey's visage SHONE;
Despite the deadly STILLNESS, he pushed the sermon ON;
He looked down at his OUTLINE, and once more the insights FLEW;
But the people still IGNORED it—even though he said...

Casey: *(Holding up two fingers)*
Point TWO!...

Reader One: *(Snoring sounds.)*
Snored the congregation, and the echo answered,
(Snoring sounds.)
But one loud...

Casey: AMEN!

Reader One: From Casey and the audience went...

**Church
Member:** *(Standing)*
WHAT?

*(Sits. **Casey**'s eyes narrow; he looks determined.)*

Reader One: They saw his face grow STERN and COLD, they saw his muscles STRAIN,
And they knew he wouldn't LET them let that TRUTH go by AGAIN.

Reader Two: The SMILE was gone from Casey's lip; his NOTES were clenched in hand;
*(**Casey** grabs notes)*
He pounded with great INTENSITY his FIST upon the STAND.
*(**Casey** pounds pulpit and mimes fervent preaching.)*
And then he started to make his POINT, and so he let it FLOW...
*(**Casey** strikes dramatic preaching pose and freezes.)*

And AFTERWARD the people told him…

**Church
Member:** (Standing)
Pastor, way to GO!

(**Church Member** sits. **Casey** holds dramatic pose for remainder of skit.)

Reader One: Oh, SOMEWHERE in this favored land the SON is shining BRIGHT;
The ORGAN'S playing somewhere, and somewhere HEARTS are LIGHT…

Reader Two: And somewhere folks are LEARNING…

Reader One: And somewhere Christians SHOUT…

Reader Two: But there is no GROWTH in MUDVILLE…

Reader One: Pastor CASEY'S been…

Reader Two: …Tuned OUT.

(Lights go down. **Casey** exits.)

▶ **Related Scriptures:**
- Psalm 119
- 1 Thessalonians 5:12-13
- 2 Timothy 3:14—4:5

▶ **Related Topics:**
- Respecting church leaders
- Qualifications of teachers
- Sincerity in worship

The Final Frontier of Alfred Centauri

Topic: Why We Need the Church

The Scene: A crewman's quarters on a star ship

The Simple Setup: Place a table and chair center stage. On the table is the "recording device" into which **Alfred** speaks most of his lines. This device need not function in any way; it could be anything from a painted piece of wood to a TV remote control. If you use a device that's large enough, such as a clipboard, it could help your actor by concealing his script. You'll also need a backpack for **Alfred**.

The Sound: If you're using stationary microphones, place one near the table and another near the door through which **Alfred** will exit. Plan his movements so that he can deliver his lines at one mike or the other. You'll need a mike offstage, too, for **Computer Voice** and for **Alfred**'s lines in the "air lock." Dress **Alfred** in an outfit reminiscent of *Star Trek*—velour-type pullover shirt and dark slacks. For the sound effect near the end of the skit, try seven to ten seconds of static recorded from a radio or TV set between stations.

Other Options: A made or borrowed real-looking *Star Trek* uniform for **Alfred** will add an additional element. Any "star ship" decorations (futuristic vase or 3-D chessboard, for example) will help also.

The Characters:
> **Alfred Centauri**, disgruntled star ship crew member
> **Computer Voice**, feminine but firm

*(As the skit begins, **Alfred** is sitting at a table, playing with a recording device.)*

Alfred:	Is this thing ON? *(He clears his throat.)* CAPTAIN'S LOG, Star Date 2217.6. **ALFRED CENTAURI** reporting. *(Pauses.)* All right, I'm NOT the captain. I'm just a CREW~MAN THIRD CLASS. But I OUGHT to be the captain! The one we have NOW is a total—Oh, REWIND! *(He clears his throat.)* PERSONAL Log, Star Date 2217.7. In this log I intend to list my HIGHLY JUSTIFIABLE GRIEVANCES—not that it will make the SLIGHTEST difference on this miserable STAR SHIP, where every CREW member aboard is a COMPLETE DISASTER. *(Pauses.)* Except ME, of course.
Computer Voice:	*(Over sound system)* ATTENTION! ATTENTION, ALL HANDS! There will be a SEMINAR on SPACE NAVIGATION, Tuesday at 1100 hours. Please mark your BIODIGITAL CAL-ENDARS. That is ALL.
Alfred:	SPACE Navigation! That's all they ever TALK about here…SPACE! What is WRONG

with these people? *(He gets up, taking the recording device with him and continuing to speak into it.)* I have been unable to find a SINGLE CLASS here on the HISTORY of MUSICAL THEATER, a subject about which NO ONE should be ignorant! Instead I find class after class about SPACE! I don't CARE about SPACE! *(He goes to an imaginary window and looks out.)* Oh, yes…we're orbiting something ROUND and ORANGE called DRACONIS FOUR. There's EXPLORING to be done…STRANGE NEW WORLDS, blah, blah, blah. I'm simply not INTO that sort of thing. But do THESE people CARE? They don't realize how FORTUNATE they are to HAVE me on this trip! There are plenty of OTHER star ships in this galaxy, you know!

Computer Voice: ATTENTION! ATTENTION, ALL HANDS! There will be a GROUP HOLOGRAM taken of the CREW this Thursday at 2200 hours. THANK you.

Alfred: *(Sarcastically)* OOH, I can hardly WAIT! What a PRIVILEGE to have my PICTURE taken with the CREW! What a PLEASURE to be counted with that pathetic collection of MISFITS! Couldn't they practice a little QUALITY CONTROL in RECRUITING? If I'd known the DREGS OF SOCIETY would be aboard, I would have stayed HOME!

Computer Voice: ATTENTION! ATTENTION, ALL HANDS! WEEKLY CREW MEETING begins in FIVE MINUTES. ALL PERSONNEL please report to the AUDITORIUM on DECK SEVEN.

Alfred: AAUGGH! CREW MEETING! The CRUELEST form of TORTURE in the known UNIVERSE! *(Into recorder)* This weekly RITUAL consists of sitting on BENCHES in the AUDITORIUM, listening to Captain WHAT'S-HIS-NAME ramble on about how GREAT it is to explore the WONDERS of space. Then they sing those INCREDIBLY DULL SONGS about the FEDERATION. As if THAT weren't enough, the captain READS from those MOLDY OLD APOLLO FLIGHT LOGS! THAT'S ENTERTAINMENT? I certainly didn't sign up for this trip to LEARN anything! I thought it was an exotic CRUISE of some sort!

Computer Voice: ATTENTION! ATTENTION, ALL HANDS! LAST CALL for CREW MEETING. This morning the captain's topic is "BOLDLY GOING WHERE NO ONE HAS GONE BEFORE."

Alfred: *(Sarcastically)* How ORIGINAL!

Computer Voice: There will also be a time for TESTIMONIALS. Over.

Alfred: Oh, the TESTIMONIALS! *(Falsetto, imitating a woman crew member)* "Space exploration is FANTASTIC! It's the best thing that ever HAPPENED to me!" *(Deep voice, imitating* *male crew member)* "My life had no MEANING until I SIGNED UP!" *(Falsetto)* "It's so GREAT to be a CREW member! The crew needs US…and we need the CREW. It's like ONE BIG LIFE SUPPORT SYSTEM!" *(Deep voice)* "I like working with the same MISSION in mind…like the parts of a WELL-OILED ION DRIVE ENGINE!" *(He returns to his own voice.)* EEWW! They've all been BRAINWASHED! And the way they sing those SONGS…especially "UPWARD STAR FLEET SOLDIERS"…

Computer Voice: ATTENTION, Crewman ALFRED CENTAURI. Please report to the TRANSPORTER ROOM at 1400 hours to BEAM DOWN to the PLANET'S SURFACE. Thank you.

Alfred: I think NOT! *(Into recorder)* I had to beam down to that awful planet's surface YESTER-DAY. When they said they wanted me for a LANDING PARTY, I expected at least a TRAY of REFRESHMENTS and a NICE LITTLE ORCHESTRA! Instead, it was some sort of LABOR! I didn't come here to WORK! *(Pauses.)* I should have KNOWN it would be a fiasco when the captain CHOSE me for this landing party. He picked me LAST, and when he DID, he called me ALBERT! Can you BELIEVE it? Only 400 PEOPLE on this ship, and he can't even remember my NAME! *(Pauses.)* And that TRANSPORTER! It beamed me next to some sort of ALIEN CACTUS, and one of the NEEDLES actually STUCK me! I was INCAPACITATED, of course. When the REST of the landing party came BACK, they told me about their great ADVENTURE, discovering ugly, smelly PLANTS and picking up boring ROCKS. *(Pauses.)* Well, this is the LAST STRAW. I simply cannot TOLERATE any more. If these drones want to SING their SONGS, GO to their MEETINGS, and WORK on their MISSION, LET them. I have BETTER things to do. I'm going to start my OWN crew…a crew of people just like ME…a crew of ONE! I'll just get my THINGS together… *(He picks up a backpack and puts it on. He continues to talk into the recorder.)* Now I'll enter the EMERGENCY EXIT AIR LOCK. *(He exits. From this point on, we hear his voice over the sound system.)* THERE we are. *(He clears his throat.)* COMPUTER! I am going to LEAVE the SHIP. Commence AIR LOCK SEQUENCE.

Computer Voice: WARNING! LEAVING THE SHIP will expose you to the VACUUM of DEEP SPACE!

Alfred: Oh, yes, I KNOW. All that NONSENSE about needing a LIFE SUPPORT SYSTEM. The DANGER of going it ALONE. All part of the BRAINWASHING! Just commence the AIR LOCK SEQUENCE!

Computer Voice: Commencing AIR LOCK SEQUENCE. EMERGENCY EXIT will open in TEN SECONDS.

Alfred: FINALLY, I'll leave all those AIRHEADS behind me! I'll be FREE! No more bother-some MEETINGS, PROGRAMS, or PEOPLE. Free at LAST! Free at LAST! Thank…

(For seven to ten seconds there is nothing but the sound of static. Then there is silence.)

Computer
Voice: ATTENTION! ATTENTION, ALL HANDS! There will be a MEMORIAL SERVICE at 2300 hours for Crewman ALFRED CENTAURI, formerly of this star ship and now...ON HIS OWN.

(The lights go out.)

▶ **Related Scriptures:**
- Romans 12:3-16
- Ephesians 4
- Hebrews 10:24-25

▶ **Related Topics:**
- Unity in the body
- Accepting one another
- Loving one another

Christianstein

Topic: Love

The Scene: A mad scientist's dungeon laboratory

The Simple Setup: You'll need a long, sturdy table, a white sheet, and basic but identifiable costumes, such as a lab coat for **Doctor** and a tattered outfit for **Igor**. There's no need to costume or make up **Christianstein** as a Frankensteinian creation; normal face and "Sunday best" will work. Props can be imaginary and pantomimed. You'll also need a clipboard and paper, a cardboard box, a pair of oven mitts, and something resembling an oversized hypodermic needle. (Use the "hypo" from a toy doctor kit, or use a cake frosting plunger or turkey baster.) For added effect, flash the platform lights for "lightning."

The Sound: If you're using stationary microphones, place two next to the table. Plan the actors' movements so they can deliver their lines at these mikes. Shake a piece of sheet metal near an offstage mike for "thunder." (Make sure **Igor** knows that the proper pronunciation for "Emil Van Gelical" is "EE-mill van JELL-ih-kull.")

Other Options: You can add tousled "fright" wigs to **Doctor** and **Igor** if available. A lab background with glassware and a "power switch" will add to the effect. For extra zing at the end of the skit, you might play the refrain from the Tina Turner song "What's Love Got To Do With It?" as the lights go down.

The Characters:
Dr. Emil Van Gelical, a very mad scientist
Igor, his shuffling ragbag of an assistant
Christianstein, a well-dressed corpse

*(As the skit begins, **Christianstein** is already lying motionless under the sheet on the table. Lightning flashes. Thunder sounds. Enter **Doctor**, carrying a clipboard. Wide-eyed and displaying a facial tic, he glances around the room. Finally he calls offstage to his assistant.)*

Doctor: IGOR! IGOR, come QUICKLY! There is much WORK to be done! *(**Doctor** goes to the table, lifts the "head" end of the sheet, looks, and makes a face as if he's going to be sick.)* IGOR! Hurry and bring the MATERIALS! *(**Doctor** busies himself checking the clipboard and adjusting imaginary controls.)*

*(Enter **Igor**, carrying a cardboard box.)*

Igor: *(Groveling, as usual)* YES, Master! HERE are the materials!

Doctor: Good, good, Igor. *(Dramatically, staring into the distance)* Now we can proceed with…THE EXPERIMENT!

(Lightning flashes. Thunder sounds.)

Igor: Oh, GOODY! I LOVE experiments…even though the VILLAGERS say you are CRAZY…

Doctor: CRAZY? CRAZY, am I? I'll show THEM who's crazy! *(His facial tic goes out of control; he slaps himself.)*

Igor: Of COURSE you will, Master. Soon the name of DOCTOR EMIL VAN GELICAL will be known throughout the PROVINCE!

Doctor: Throughout the WORLD, Igor!

Igor: YES, Master. Perhaps your FAME would have spread SOONER if you hadn't BOR-ROWED the BURGHERMEISTER'S BRAIN before he was FINISHED with it…

Doctor: SILENCE, Igor! Let us not DWELL on the PAST. TONIGHT I will conduct the greatest EXPERIMENT of my CAREER. It will be…my ultimate TRIUMPH!

Igor: OOH! I LOVE triumphs!

Doctor: TONIGHT I am going to achieve what NO MAN has done BEFORE. Tonight I create… SPIRITUAL LIFE! *(Lightning flashes. Thunder sounds.)* This is my FINEST HOUR, Igor! For tonight I create…CHRISTIANSTEIN!

(Lightning flashes. Thunder sounds.)

Igor: C-C-CHRISTIANSTEIN?

Doctor: *(Grasping **Igor** by the shoulders)* YES, my misshapen friend. Let them call me a MADMAN, an EVIL GENIUS, a TAMPERER with NATURE. TONIGHT I shall prove them WRONG. CHRISTIANSTEIN will be the GREATEST SPECIMEN OF SPIRITUAL LIFE the world has ever KNOWN! He'll have EVERYTHING, Igor. He'll be…the PER-FECT CHRISTIAN!

(Lightning flashes. Thunder sounds.)

Igor: *(Looking around for source of thunder and lightning)* Could they stop DOING that? It's making me NERVOUS.

Doctor: Very WELL, Igor. Let the operation BEGIN! *(**Doctor** pulls the sheet from the table, un-covering the inanimate form of a man dressed in a white shirt, tie, and dark suit.)* IGOR! Give me my SURGICAL GLOVES!

Igor: *(Handing him a pair of oven mitts)* YES, Master. *(**Doctor** puts on the mitts, then proceeds with the operation, his back to the audience. As **Doctor** calls for various items, **Igor** finds them in the box and hands them over, palming them so that the audience can't tell they're imaginary.)*

Doctor: SCALPEL! *(Pauses.)* SPONGE! *(Pauses.)* FORCEPS! *(Pauses.)* CLAMP! *(Pauses.)* FOREHEAD!

Igor: *(Looking in box)* But I don't SEE a FOREHEAD, master. Are you SURE…

Doctor: I mean WIPE MY FOREHEAD, Igor! I'm SWEATING!

Igor: *(Wiping **Doctor**'s forehead)* Oh. Sorry.

Doctor: And now, it is time to EQUIP my creation! Give me the VOICE OF A GREAT EVANGELIST, Igor!

Igor: YES, master!

Doctor: The COURAGE of STEPHEN!

Igor: Yes, YES, master!

Doctor: The PATIENCE of JOB!

Igor: *(So excited he forgets to follow the order)* Yes, yes, yes, yes, YES!

Doctor: I said, the PATIENCE OF JOB! HURRY IT UP, Igor!

Igor: Oh. Sorry. *(He hands over the item.)*

Doctor: Now, the HYPODERMIC NEEDLE.

Igor: *(Pulling it from the box)* OOH! It's a BIG one!

Doctor: And the SERUMS I distilled. *(**Igor** presents the box; **Doctor** will use hypodermic to withdraw fluids that are supposedly in the box and inject them into **Christianstein**.)* First, I'll give him DOUBLE DOSES of DAILY PRAYER AND BIBLE READING…then FAITHFUL CHURCH ATTENDANCE…generous GIVING…TEMPERANCE…VOLUNTEER work…ability to resist TEMPTATION…WITNESSING…and LAST, but not LEAST, a TRIPLE INJECTION of…ORTHODOXY!

*(Lightning flashes. Thunder sounds. **Igor** cringes.)*

Doctor: *(Checking his clipboard list)* Examine the BOX, Igor. Have we FORGOTTEN anything?

Igor: *(Looking into box)* Oh, NO, Master. Everything must be in PLACE!

Doctor: EXCELLENT! *(He yanks off the oven mitts.)* Now to fasten the POWER CABLES. *(He appears to do so.)* THIS is the moment the world has WAITED for. This is the moment for…CHRISTIANSTEIN! *(Lightning flashes. Thunder sounds. Igor puts his hands over his ears.)* A MILLION VOLTS OF LIGHTNING will bring my creation to LIFE. *(Doctor goes to a real or imaginary switch on the wall.)* Now STAND BACK while I throw the POWER SWITCH! Prepare to meet the PERFECT CHRISTIAN…CHRISTIANSTEIN!

*(Lightning flashes. Thunder sounds. **Igor** wraps his arms around his head. The **Doctor** throws the switch as lightning and thunder continue. Then, as lightning and thunder subside, the figure on the table begins to twitch.)*

Igor: MASTER! He's—he's MOVING!

Doctor: YES, Igor, YES! My creation is…ALIVE!

*(They watch breathlessly as **Christianstein** slowly sits up, then stiffly gets off the table and stands.)*

Igor: OOH! You've DONE it, Master! He's the PERFECT CHRISTIAN!

Doctor: OH, my CREATION! SPEAK to me!

*(**Christianstein** frowns. Finally he speaks in a low and hostile growl.)*

Christianstein: If I speak in the tongues of MEN and of ANGELS, but have not LOVE…

Doctor: *(Scanning clipboard)* LOVE?

Christianstein: *(Raising his arms toward **Doctor**, who continues to consult list)* If I have the GIFT of PROPHECY and can fathom all MYSTERIES and all KNOWLEDGE, and if I have a FAITH that can move MOUNTAINS, but have not LOVE…

Doctor: LOVE? Igor, what's LOVE got to do with it?

Igor: I—I don't KNOW, Master! *(He hides under the table.)*

Christianstein: If I give all I POSSESS to the POOR and surrender my BODY to the FLAMES, but have not LOVE…*(he grabs **Doctor** by the collar)* I…gain…NOTHING!

Doctor: N-NOTHING? N-not even a LITTLE something?

Christianstein: AARRGGHH!

Doctor: *(Fleeing as **Christianstein** lumbers after him)* IGOR, you fool! I KNEW we'd left SOMETHING out!

Christianstein: AARRGGHH‼

Doctor: Such a LITTLE thing... *(He runs off, followed by **Christianstein**.)*

*(There is a pause. Finally **Igor** crawls out from under the table.)*

Igor: I-I think we've created...a MONSTER!

*(Lightning flashes. Thunder sounds. **Igor** runs out, his hands over his ears.)*

► **Related Scriptures:**
- Romans 13:8-10
- I Corinthians 13
- I John 3

► **Related Topics:**
- Spiritual gifts
- Human effort versus grace
- Our standards and God's standards

Waiting for the Ambulance

Topic: Christ's Return

The Scene: Along an isolated highway at night

The Simple Setup: No set is required. **Old Persons 1** and **2** will need calculators.

The Sound: Lapel or wireless microphones will free the actors to scatter about the stage and deliver their lines while lying down, sitting, or standing. If wireless mikes are not available, use four hand-held mikes without stands. Place them on the stage, widely spaced—one for **Woman**, one for **Man**, one for **Old Persons** to share, and one for **Young Person** to pick up when he or she enters. When **Driver** enters, he can use any microphone. You'll also need a siren sound effect.

Other Options: For added atmosphere, a revolving, flashing red or blue light will add effect when the ambulance arrives near the end of the skit. To suggest an outdoor scene at night, you can cast a blue light on the stage. A road sign and/or scattered auto parts, such as tires, a bumper, and so on, will help add realism to the skit.

The Characters:
Young Person, levelheaded but exhausted
Woman, worried and fussy
Man, gruff and independent
Old Person 1, contentious and nit-picking
Old Person 2, just like **Old Person 1**
Driver, compassionate but matter-of-fact

*(As the skit begins, there is just enough light to see four bodies—**Woman**, **Man**, and **Old Persons 1** and 2—lying on the stage. After a few moments some groans are heard.)*

Woman:		*(Slowly sitting up)* Oohh—What HAPPENED?
Man:		*(Also sitting up)* What do you THINK happened? A FOUR-CAR PILEUP! *(He points offstage.)* My PONTIAC! It looks like a KIA!
Woman:		Oh, the HEM of my DRESS is just RUINED! How will I EVER get this awful ASPHALT STAIN out?
Old Person 1:		*(Slowly sitting up)* Oohh…my ARM! I think my TIBIA is broken!
Old Person 2:		*(Also sitting up)* That's not your TIBIA! Your tibia is in your LEG!

Old Person 1: It is NOT! That's my FIBULA!

Man: Where's the OTHER driver? I want to know EVERYONE'S INSURANCE COMPANY!

Old Person 2: *(To Old Person 1)* I NEVER should have let you DRIVE! You're BLIND as a BAT!

Old Person 1: And YOU have the MEMORY of a FRUIT FLY! YOU were driving...and EXCEEDING the SPEED LIMIT by 29 MILES PER HOUR, I might add!

(Young Person enters, limping.)

Young Person: *(Breathing hard)* It's...OK. There was a PHONE BOOTH about a HUNDRED YARDS down the ROAD. I talked to the AMBULANCE DRIVER. He'll be out to GET us very SOON.

Woman: *(Working on her dress)* Not TOO soon, I hope! I simply MUST fix this DRESS!

Man: How do you KNOW this so-called AMBULANCE DRIVER is coming? I don't believe he IS!

Young Person: He PROMISED he would!

Man: HMPH!

Old Person 1: *(To Young Person)* Tell me, EXACTLY what did the ambulance driver SAY?

Old Person 2: YES! We must know his EXACT WORDS!

Young Person: He said, "STAY OFF the ROAD and KEEP ALERT. Don't let anyone DOZE OFF. I'm about 31 MILES AWAY. I PROMISE I'll be there as SOON as I CAN." And that was IT.

Old Person 1: HMM. He said 31 MILES. *(Pulls out a calculator and pushes buttons.)* Let's see...average SPEED, 55. I figure he will arrive in EXACTLY 34 MINUTES AND 24 SECONDS!

Old Person 2: *(Taking out a calculator and pushing buttons)* You're WRONG, as USUAL! It's 33 MINUTES AND 48 SECONDS!

Old Person 1: BALDERDASH! You're not allowing for the HUNDRED YARDS between the PHONE BOOTH and our PRESENT POSITION!

Old Person 2: I am SO!

Young Person: Hold ON, please! The AMBULANCE DRIVER didn't say WHEN he would get here, only that he WOULD! That's the IMPORTANT thing, isn't it?

(Old Persons lower their voices but keep arguing.)

Woman: Oh, MY! Just 33 or 34 MINUTES! How am I EVER going to fix this DRESS before he gets here? *(She rummages in her purse.)* I've got SO much to DO!

Man: He won't get here at ALL! I can't wait here FOREVER. I'm going to get help MYSELF! *(He pulls himself to his feet and staggers in the direction opposite from the phone booth.)*

Young Person: WAIT! He'll be HERE! I KNOW it!

Man: HA!

Young Person: But you're going the WRONG WAY!

Man: I can take care of MYSELF, kid! *(He exits.)*

Old Person 1: I've GOT it! That ambulance driver said, "STAY OFF THE ROAD." There's a HIDDEN MEANING there, if you STUDY IT CLOSELY. It means the ambulance will not arrive on the ROAD at ALL, but out there in the TREES!

Old Person 2: No, in the HILLS!

Old Person 1: The TREES!

Old Person 2: Stop ARGUING! The IMPORTANT thing is to GET AWAY from the road IMMEDIATELY!

(Old Persons slowly get to their feet.)

Young Person: WAIT! He didn't mean we were to LEAVE THE ROAD!

Old Person 1: *(Shaking his head)* I'm afraid you have not STUDIED the driver's STATEMENT as WE have!

Old Person 2: There are MYSTERIES here that you cannot COMPREHEND!

Old Person 1: NAMES!

Old Person 2: PLACES!

Old Person 1: DATES!

Old Person 2: TIMES!

Old Person 1: *(To Old Person 2)* Now, remember to LISTEN for the SIGN...the AMBULANCE SIREN!

Old Person 2: No, keep an EYE out for the FLASHING RED LIGHT!

Old Person 1: SIREN!

Old Person 2: LIGHT!

(They exit, arguing.)

Young Person: *(After a pause)* MA'AM? Are you still THERE?

Woman: *(Trying to fix hem of dress)* YES, but I'm VERY BUSY! I've got a MILLION things to DO before he GETS here, and I don't want to be DISTURBED!

(Young Person sits center stage, staring straight ahead.)

Young Person: Got to...stay AWAKE. Got to...keep ALERT. It's so COLD...so COLD... *(Folds arms, trying to stay warm. After several seconds, a distant siren is heard. The sound rouses Young Person.)* HEY! Do you HEAR that? It's the AMBULANCE! It HAS to be!

Woman: Oh, NO, NO! He CAN'T come YET! I'm not DONE! *(She looks around, frantic.)* I've got to HIDE! He can come back and get me LATER! I've just GOT to finish this DRESS! *(She gets up and stumbles toward exit.)*

Young Person: Ma'am, WAIT! He's almost HERE! You can't...

Woman: Don't let him FIND me! I'm not READY yet! *(She exits.)*

(Siren gets louder, then stops. Driver enters and looks around.)

Young Person: You—you MADE it!

Driver: Of COURSE! *(He helps Young Person up.)* But...what happened to the OTHERS?

Young Person: They...LEFT. Some didn't BELIEVE...some weren't READY...some got too INVOLVED in something ELSE...

Driver: *(Nodding)* Yeah. It HAPPENS. *(He starts to help Young Person toward exit, but Young Person stops.)*

Young Person: Say…that's a pretty SMALL AMBULANCE, isn't it? I mean, you couldn't get a whole lot of PEOPLE in there…

Driver: *(Nodding)* That's TRUE. *(Pauses.)* But then, there weren't a whole lot of people left WAITING for me, WERE there?

(They exit.)

▶ **Related Scriptures:**
- Matthew 25:1-13
- John 14:1-4
- 2 Peter 3

▶ **Related Topics:**
- Prophecy
- Preparing for eternity
- Serving God while there's time

I Don't Read the Cookbook Anymore

Topic: Bible Reading

The Scene: A TV studio

The Simple Setup: To set the stage for a TV cooking show set, place a few culinary items (pots and pans, mixing bowl and spoon, rolling pin, for example) on a table at center stage. **Sean** and **Sherry** should wear casual clothes befitting their characters, plus aprons. Chefs hats will add a nice touch and can be purchased at a kitchen accessory store.

The Sound: If you're using stationary microphones, set up one behind the table for each of the actors.

Other Options: To add realism to your cooking show set, set up a VHS camcorder on a tripod, either with or without a camera operator, and point it at the actors.

The Characters:
>   **Chef Sean**, a surfer dude
>   **Chef Sherry**, a Valley girl
>   **Camera Operator** (optional)

*(As the lights come up, **Sean** and **Sherry** stand at a table that's laden with culinary items. If you have included a camera and an operator, he or she should be in place as well.)*

Sherry: SO, are we ON? COOL! Well, like, HI, and welcome to "THE CLUELESS GOURMET"... the NEW PROGRAM that tells you, like, how to COOK stuff! I'm CHEF SHERRY...

Sean: And I'm, like, CHEF SEAN. SO, like, SHERRY, since this is our FIRST SHOW, I wonder whether you'd tell our VIEWERS how you became a CHEF.

Sherry: Oh, that would be TOTALLY COOL!

Sean: *(After a long pause)* So, like, GO AHEAD!

Sherry: OH! RIGHT! Well, it was really the COOKBOOK that got me STARTED.

Sean: AH! The COOKBOOK!

Sherry: This GUY on, like, a STREET CORNER gave me a copy. It was so BIG...with a LEATHER COVER, and GOLD EDGES on the pages, and this cloth BOOKMARK that HUNG OUT...sort of like a CUTE LITTLE TONGUE...

Sean: COOL!

Sherry: ANYWAY, I took the cookbook HOME and looked at all the RECIPES...SALSA, STIR FRY, SNICKERDOODLES...

Sean: SNICKERDOODLES! YUM, YUM!

Sherry: I, like, REALLY wanted to be able to make all those TOTALLY MOUTH-WATERING DISHES. When I got to the part that tells how to become a CHEF...I just FOLLOWED DIRECTIONS!

Sean: What a RADICAL day THAT must have been!

Sherry: Oh, like, you are SO RIGHT! From then on I spent EVERY SPARE MINUTE reading that cookbook. I carried it under my ARM wherever I went, even though it didn't even MATCH MY PURSE!

Sean: WOW!

Sherry: People would, like, ASK me about that book I was carrying, and I'd tell them the WHOLE STORY. I wanted EVERYONE to become a chef!

Sean: For SURE!

Sherry: But after a while I got TIRED of lugging that HEAVY BOOK around all the time. So I left it HOME...being careful not to put, like, any OTHER books on TOP of it, of course.

Sean: Oh, I HEAR ya!

Sherry: I kept READING a little of the cookbook every DAY. But then I noticed, like, how BORING some of it is. Like the FIRST part, telling the whole HISTORY OF COOKING. I mean, WHO needs to know THAT? This is, like, the 20TH CENTURY!

Sean: RIGHT! We've got MICROWAVES now, not...whatever they USED to use.

Sherry: I LOVED the cookbook, but that FIRST part was...well...BOGUS!

Sean: BOGUS! YEAH!

Sherry: Besides, I was too BUSY to read. There was so much COOKING to do, you know? So anyway, I joined the COOKING SOCIETY, and all the other chefs thought my PESTO PASTA with SUN-DRIED TOMATOES and ARTICHOKE BOTTOMS was to DIE for!

Sean: Sounds TOTALLY TASTY!

Sherry: I didn't have time to cook AND read. So I started cooking WITHOUT the book!

Sean: EXTREME!

Sherry: It was, like, NO PROBLEM! After all, I'd already READ most of the popular RECIPES. I'd heard LECTURES at the COOKING SOCIETY. What ELSE did I need?

Sean: Beats ME! So, was your new plan a SUCCESS?

Sherry: TOTALLY! Well, SORT of. A few people didn't like my LICORICE BURRITOS.

Sean: SMALL MINDS, Sherry. SMALL MINDS!

Sherry: You are, like, SO PERCEPTIVE! ANYWAY, after a while, I'd cooked WITHOUT THE COOKBOOK so long that I couldn't remember ANY of it. I couldn't FIND MY COPY either, so I MADE THINGS UP as I went along.

Sean: How totally CREATIVE!

Sherry: Once I made CHOCOLATE CHIP COOKIES you could DRINK through a STRAW.

Sean: MM! DIGESTABLE!

Sherry: Well, some of my FELLOW CHEFS at the COOKING SOCIETY didn't think so. They started pestering me to "GET BACK INTO THE BOOK." They even wanted me to MEMORIZE parts of the cookbook and FOLLOW its INSTRUCTIONS!

Sean: UNBELIEVABLE!

Sherry: Naturally, I QUIT the Cooking Society. Once in a while I'd buy a MAGAZINE about DIETING. Or I'd watch one of those COOKING SHOWS on TV.

Sean: Like THIS one!

Sherry: RIGHT! Finally I stopped hanging around the kitchen ALTOGETHER. These days I don't DO much COOKING. If I get, like, totally HUNGRY I'll warm up a TV DINNER...but the old EXCITEMENT just isn't there.

Sean: WOW! What an INSPIRING STORY!

Sherry: SO, like, what are we going to DO on the show today?

Sean: Well, I think we just DID it. We are, like, SO OUT OF TIME!

Sherry: BUMMER!

Sean: So tune in NEXT week, folks, when we'll show you how to...BOIL WATER!

Sherry: Um...BOIL WATER? Couldn't we start with something EASIER? Like...how to turn on the FAUCET?

Sean: What's the MATTER, Sherry? Can't remember how to BOIL WATER?

Sherry: Oh, that is SO NOT FAIR! OF COURSE I can remember how to BOIL WATER! *(Pauses.)* I just can't remember WHY.

Sean: THAT'S cool! Neither can I! Thanks for WATCHING, everybody!

Sherry: And don't FORGET...

Unison: STAY CLUELESS!

(The lights go off; the actors exit.)

▶ **Related Scriptures:**

- Deuteronomy 6:6–9
- 2 Timothy 2:15
- Acts 17:11

▶ **Related Topics:**

- Faithfulness
- Spiritual disciplines
- Losing your "first love"

The Devil's Advocate

Topic: Temptation

The Scene: Outside a bank

The Simple Setup: No special set is needed. **Softsell** will need a briefcase, business cards, and a cigar; he should be dressed in a sharp suit. **Man** and **Woman** may wear casual dress.

The Sound: If you're using stationary microphones, put two of them center stage. You'll need a siren sound effect as well.

Other Options: For added atmosphere, use a revolving, flashing red or blue light to add effect while the siren is heard near the skit's end. (Feel free to update **Softsell**'s line referring to his celebrity clients, using names currently in the news.)

The Characters:
>**Lionel Softsell**, a cocky, smooth-talking shyster reminiscent of the late Phil Hartman's overconfident but inept lawyer on *The Simpsons*
>**Man**, average but unsure of himself
>**Woman**, average but naive

(Man approaches imaginary building, center stage. He looks it over, seeming to ponder something. Softsell enters with a briefcase, watches for a moment, then speaks in a flattering yet insincere manner.)

Softsell:		So…planning to ROB the BANK, eh?
Man:		*(Startled)* What? NO! I'm just using the ATM!
Softsell:		*(With a knowing laugh and way too much familiarity)* Uh-huh. HEY, my friend…I won't tell if YOU won't! *(He gives Man a big wink.)*
Man:		REALLY, I'm just…
Softsell:		*(Taking out a business card and giving it to Man)* Let me INTRODUCE myself, compadre. I'm LIONEL SOFTSELL, ATTORNEY-AT-LAW. I'll be GLAD to give you LEGAL ADVICE while you plan your big HEIST!
Man:		HEIST? I'm not a BANK ROBBER!
Softsell:		You don't LIKE money?
Man:		Well, of COURSE I…

Softsell: Money TALKS, my friend…and right now it's calling your NAME! *(Calling softly)* "JOE! JOE!"

Man: My name's BOB.

Softsell: Just TESTING! So, Bill, how about HELPING YOURSELF to that GREENBACK BUFFET?

Man: THAT would be STEALING!

Softsell: "STEALING"—what a HARSH word. I prefer to call it…STRATEGIC RESOURCE DIVERSION!

Man: HUH?

Softsell: It's a LEGAL term. Now, just put yourself in MY hands, *mon ami*, and you can be RICH beyond your wildest DREAMS!

Man: But I'd get CAUGHT!

Softsell: That's what they'd LIKE you to believe!

Man: THEY?

Softsell: The POWER brokers…the ELITE…the ALIENS from PLANET X!

Man: ALIENS?

Softsell: It's a LEGAL term, Ed. SO, what'll it BE? A bit of the DO-RE-MI for do-re-YOU?

Man: I don't want to go to JAIL!

Softsell: *(Chuckling)* JAIL? My friend, if I could guarantee that you wouldn't spend a MINUTE in jail, would you grab those BUCKS, that MOOLA, those SIMOLEONS?

Man: Well…

Softsell: Of COURSE you would!

Man: Are you saying nobody would find OUT? I would never get CAUGHT?

Softsell: As surely as I know the BACK of my HAND! *(To himself, looking at the back of his hand)* Hmm…what is THAT?

Man: But what if I get ARRESTED?

Softsell: No PROBLEMO. You just take the FOURTH!

Man: Take the FOURTH amendment? Isn't that the one about SEARCHES and SEIZURES?

Softsell: Uh...RIGHT. That OTHER one is so...OVERDONE.

Man: Are you SURE you're a real lawyer?

Softsell: My friend, I'm WAY past that. I'm a CELEBRITY lawyer!

Man: REALLY? Who are some of your CLIENTS?

Softsell: I'm afraid that's CONFIDENTIAL. I can only give you INITIALS. Let's see...MIKE TYSON would be M.T....HUGH GRANT would be H.G....MARV ALBERT would be M.A....

Man: WOW, all those guys are FAMOUS! I guess you MUST know what you're talking about!

Softsell: BELIEVE me, amigo, I've been doing this for a VERY long time. SO, are you READY?

Man: OK! Here I GO! *(He walks offstage.* ***Softsell*** *takes out a cigar and admires it as a siren wails. He puts the cigar in his mouth. Siren fades out, and* ***Softsell*** *takes out the cigar.)*

Softsell: Sometimes it's just TOO EASY.

*(****Woman*** *enters and looks at another imaginary building.* ***Softsell*** *puts cigar back in his pocket.)*

Softsell: SO...that's quite a BAKERY, isn't it?

Woman: WHAT? Oh, YES!

Softsell: How about some of those DELICIOUS DONUTS?

Woman: Oh, I CAN'T. They're LOADED with CALORIES!

Softsell: CALORIES? Such a HARSH word. I prefer to call them NUTRITIONAL PLEASURE UNITS!

Woman: PLEASURE units?

Softsell: It's a LEGAL term. *(Leading her offstage.)* Allow me to INTRODUCE myself...

Related Scriptures:
- Genesis 3
- 1 Corinthians 10:12-13
- James 1:13-15

Related Topics:
- Spiritual warfare
- The love of money

Hailing the Chief

Topic: Prayer

The Scene: The Oval Office

The Simple Setup: At center stage you'll need a desk with a chair behind it and a "guest" chair nearby. If you have an American flag on a stand, set it next to the desk. On the desk you'll need something resembling an intercom. (A clock radio facing away from the audience will work.) The **President** can use the intercom by pretending to push a button on it and speaking toward it. When the **Secretary**'s voice is heard through the intercom, it's actually coming from an offstage microphone. Put some papers and a pen on the desk. **President**, **Secretary**, and **Formal Man** should wear suits; **Young Woman**, bathrobe and hair curlers; **Elderly Man**, golfing outfit; and the rest, casual clothes. Other props include a pocket stereo for **Teenager** and piece of paper for **Elderly Man**.

The Sound: If you're using stationary microphones, put one offstage for use by **Narrator** and for **Secretary** when she's not on stage. In addition, place one on the desk and one nearby to be used by the petitioners. If possible, give **Crawling Man** a hand-held mike to carry.

Other Options: To act out the skit using a smaller cast, let some of your actors play more than one part. For example, one male actor could appear as **Formal Man**, **Crawling Man**, and **Elderly Man**—as long as he can change costumes quickly. One female actor could play the roles of **Housewife** and **Young Woman**.

The Characters:
> **Narrator**, warm-voiced
> **President**, down-to-earth despite his power
> **Secretary**, businesslike but respectful
> **Housewife**, oblivious to her surroundings, with a nasal, singsong voice
> **Formal Man**, a melodramatic blowhard with a booming voice
> **Crawling Man**, a cringing groveler
> **Teenager**, perpetually moving and absorbed in his music
> **Elderly Man**, brusque and peevish
> **Young Woman**, on the verge of sleep
> **Boy**, eight to ten years old, wide-eyed and polite

*(As the lights come up, the **President** signs papers at his desk. As **Narrator** speaks, **President** looks up and smiles, then scratches his chin as if deep in thought.)*

Narrator: He sat at his DESK in the OVAL OFFICE, waiting. He WAITED even though there were a STACK OF LETTERS TO SIGN, a CABLE TO READ, a PRESS CONFERENCE TO PRE-PARE FOR, a BRIEFING WITH THE CABINET TO ATTEND, a TEA FOR AN AMBASSA-DOR IN THE ROSE GARDEN…*(Pauses.)* Looking up from his SCHEDULE, he SMILED. Yes, there WAS a lot to do. But first some PEOPLE were coming…some very IMPOR-TANT people. *(Pauses.)* At least HE thought they were very important. That was why he kept INVITING them to COME to the Oval Office and TALK with him. He LONGED TO HEAR what was in their HEARTS and MINDS, to TALK about how they FELT, what they NEEDED, how they could help him ACCOMPLISH his GOALS...

Secretary: *(Offstage, as if through intercom)* Mr. PRESIDENT?

President: Yes?

Secretary: They're HERE, sir.

President: AH! Send the first one IN, please. *(He leans forward in his chair, waiting.)*

(Housewife enters. President offers his hand, but she ignores it and plops down in chair. She shuts her eyes tight.)

Housewife: *(Singsong voice)* DEAR MR. PRESIDENT...THANK you for the world so SWEET, THANK you for the FOOD we eat, THANK you for the BIRDS that sing, THANK you, sir, for EVERYTHING. GOODBYE. *(She opens her eyes, gets up, and exits. President makes a move as if to say something, but then he just sighs. After a pause he pushes the intercom button.)*

President: NEXT, please.

(Formal Man enters. He ignores President's offered hand. Formal Man plants himself near the desk, clasps his hands, and looks at the ceiling.)

Formal Man: O thou CHIEF EXECUTIVE who art in the WHITE HOUSE...O thou in whom so much doth constitutionally DWELL, upon whose DESK hath been placed a most effective BLOTTER; incline thine EAR toward thy most humble CITIZEN, and grant that thy many ENTITIES may be manifoldly ENDOWED upon the fruitful PLAIN...*(President winces, closes his eyes, and rubs his temples.)* And may thy THOU dost HARKENETH whatly didst shalt EVERMORE in twain ASUNDER!

President: EXCUSE me...but WHAT...

Formal Man: GOODBYE. *(He exits.)*

President: *(Sighing and pushing intercom button)* Next, please.

(Crawling Man enters on his hands and knees. President stares at him.)

Crawling Man: *(Not looking up)* Oh, Mr. G-GREAT AND AWFUL P-PRESIDENT! I am but a DISGUSTING piece of FILTH in your presence. No, I am LESS than that! How DARE I enter here? How DARE I think that you would do ANYTHING but GRIND me into the FLOOR?

President: *(Offering his hand)* Please, get UP. You don't have to do THAT. I WANT to talk with you!

Crawling Man: *(Still groveling)* I deserve only to be SQUASHED under the WEIGHT of your mighty DESK! I could NEVER have received an invitation to talk with YOU. It MUST have been a MISTAKE. How can you ever FORGIVE me for breaking IN like this? Oh, I'm so SORRY, so SORRY, so SORRY! *(He crawls out, groaning.)*

(President shakes his head. Finally he pushes the intercom button.)

President: Next.

(Teenager enters, wearing headphones and bobbing up and down to the music of his pocket stereo.)

Teenager: *(Ignoring offered hand of the President)* HEY, Prez! What's HAPPENING? Nice PLACE you've got here. I'm, like, SO glad we could have this little CHAT, you know? You're not BAD for an OLD dude, I guess. You don't bother ME, I won't bother YOU, OK? Well, I've gotta GO. Hang IN there! *(Teenager exits.)*

(President drums his fingers on the desk. He pushes intercom button.)

President: NEXT, please.

(Elderly Man enters, staring at a piece of paper he's holding. He ignores the President's offered hand.)

Elderly Man: *(Not looking up from his list)* Mr. President, I want there to be a PARKING SPACE waiting for me when I go DOWNTOWN this afternoon. Not a PARALLEL parking space, either…one I can drive right INTO. And not one with a PARKING METER. YOU can see to it that none of those METER MAIDS gives me a TICKET. Now, this is IMPORTANT!

President: *(After clearing his throat politely)* Speaking of IMPORTANT…how do you feel about my program to FEED the HUNGRY? Would you like to have a PART in…

Elderly Man: *(Still staring at list)* And ANOTHER thing! I lost my best GOLF CLUB. A PUTTER. Can't remember where I PUT it. Now, you FIND it for me, WILL you? Got to have that club before SATURDAY! I KNOW you can DO it. GOODBYE!

(Elderly Man shuffles out the door. President slumps in his chair. Finally he pushes intercom button.)

President: NEXT!

(After a pause, Young Woman enters slowly. She looks like a sleepwalker—eyes nearly shut, jaw slack, her feet dragging. She yawns and slides into chair.)

Young Woman: *(Nodding off)* Dear…Mr.…President…I KNOW I should talk to you when I'm more… AWAKE…but I've got SO many things to do…So…SLEEPY…There was something I was going to SAY…I was going to…*(She starts snoring. **President** pushes intercom button.)*

President: Uh, BARBARA?

Secretary: YES, Mr. President?

President: Could you help this young lady OUT?

Secretary: CERTAINLY, Mr. President. *(**Secretary** enters and helps the dozing **Young Woman** to her feet.)*

President: How many do we have LEFT?

Secretary: I'm SORRY, sir. But as USUAL, MOST of the people you sent INVITATIONS to said they were too BUSY to talk. They had to WATCH TV, WAX THE CAR, DO the DISHES…

President: Oh. *(Pauses.)* Isn't ANYONE else out there?

Secretary: There is ONE, sir. But you wouldn't want to talk with HIM.

President: Why NOT?

Secretary: Because he's…just a CHILD, Mr. President.

President: *(Shrugging)* You may as well show him IN.

Secretary: Very WELL, Sir. *(**Secretary** supports dozing **Young Woman** as the two of them exit. After a moment, **Boy** enters shyly. He looks around the room, his eyes wide.)*

Boy: Are—are you REALLY the PRESIDENT?

President: I really AM. *(He offers his hand; **Boy** reaches up and shakes it. **Boy** then sits, folds his hands, and waits.)*

*(**President** sits and watches **Boy** for a long pause, his eyebrows raised. Finally **President** speaks.)*

President: Isn't there…something you want to TELL me? Something you have to RECITE, or ASK FOR, or SAY?

*(**Boy** looks down, thinking. Then he looks up.)*

Boy: YES. I guess there IS.

President: Okay... What IS it?

Boy: THANK you for INVITING me. *(Pauses.)* THAT'S all.

*(**President** looks dumbfounded. Then a smile spreads across his face.)*

Narrator: When the President heard THAT, he couldn't seem to SAY anything for a while. All he could do was SMILE. But then they TALKED and TALKED and TALKED for the LONGEST, most WONDERFUL time.

(The lights fade out.)

▶ **Related Scriptures:**
- Matthew 6:5-14
- Philippians 4:4-7
- Hebrews 4:14-16

▶ **Related Topics:**
- God's interest in us
- Putting God's kingdom first
- Having a personal relationship with God

The Man Who Built His House Upon a Rock

Topic: Faithfulness

The Scene: A beach

The Simple Setup: Two cardboard house shapes are needed. They may be decorated elaborately or not at all. The base of **Man**'s house should be colored rock gray; the base of **Neighbor**'s house should be sand brown. Cover the rock-based house with a sheet that can be removed. The rock-based house must be large enough for **Man** to hide behind; the sand-based house should be large enough to conceal **Neighbor** and **Friends**. The rock-based house could be fastened to a table for support; the sand-based house must be pulled over by the actors at the end, so you may want to fasten it to a chair or two. Practice the crash at the end beforehand to make sure the actors understand how to pull the house down. **Man** will need an umbrella and a suitcase; **Neighbor** and **Friends** will need sand pails and shovels, drinking glasses, a hammer, and a sign that says, "COMING SOON: LUXURY BEACHFRONT RESORT." The sign should be made so it can be attached to the sand-based house. (Use tape or Velcro fastener.) All actors can wear casual clothes; **Neighbor** and **Friends** might wear tropical print shirts or other "fun-at-the-beach" outfits.

The Sound: If you're using stationary microphones, place one in front of the rock-based house, slightly to the center-stage side of the house, so that **Man** can deliver his lines while peeking out from behind the house as well as standing in front of it. **Narrator** and **Weatherman** can share an off-stage mike. For sound effects you'll need hammering (hammer a wood block), thunder (shake a piece of sheet metal or use recorded thunder), and a crash (drop some pieces of lumber into a large box or use a recorded crash).

Other Options: If you have an entrance door at each side of the platform, you may want to position one house in front of each door, attaching each house to the door frame or wall, which may be easier than getting the houses to stand on their own.

The Characters:

    Narrator, dignified but not stuffy
    Man, self-righteous and given to mood swings
    Neighbor, friendly and animated
    Friend One, a party animal
    Friend Two, another party animal
    Weatherman, a smooth radio voice

*(As the skit begins, there are two cardboard house shapes on stage. **Neighbor** is hidden behind sand-based house.)*

Narrator: BEHOLD, there was a MAN who built his HOUSE upon a ROCK. *(Man enters and pulls the sheet from the rock-based house, then looks at it proudly.)*

Man: *(Chuckling)* Oh, how WISE I am to build my HOUSE upon a ROCK! And how FOOLISH is the man next DOOR *(points at other house)* who built HIS house upon the SAND! For it is WRITTEN that when the RAIN descends and the FLOODS come and the WINDS blow and BEAT upon these houses, the one founded upon the ROCK will FALL NOT. But GREAT will be the FALL of the house built upon the SAND! Oh, HA, HA, HA!

Narrator: And so laughing, the man who built his house upon a ROCK went into his house and LOCKED the DOOR. *(**Man** goes behind rock-based house.)*

Man: *(Peeking from around the edge of his house)* Now I will RELAX and wait for the STORM WARNINGS…for MY house is founded SAFE upon a ROCK!

Narrator: And so he DID wait. And he WAITED and WAITED. *(Pauses.)* And nothing HAPPENED. There was no RAIN, no FLOOD, no WIND…not even a mild DRIZZLE.

Man: *(Coming out from behind house)* Hey, WAIT a minute! There's supposed to be a big STORM, and the house built upon the SAND is supposed to fall DOWN! EVERY-BODY knows THAT!

Narrator: *(**Man** peers skyward.)* So he WATCHED the SKY, hoping for a HURRICANE…or at least a major HAILSTORM. But there was NOTHING.

Man: Well, I'm SURE that STORM will come along any MINUTE now. In the MEAN-TIME, that man who built his house upon the SAND must be pretty NERVOUS! I'll bet he's having a TERRIBLE time in that FLIMSY LITTLE HOUSE of his!

*(**Man** chuckles smugly as **Neighbor** enters from behind sand-based house carrying child's beach pail and shovel. **Neighbor** happily begins to mime making sand castles. **Man** frowns. **Neighbor** beckons to someone offstage. **Friends One** and **Two** enter with similar pails and shovels and happily join **Neighbor** in his fun.)*

Man: This is OUTRAGEOUS! Those people should be MISERABLE, not happy. They should be BEGGING for shelter in MY house, hoping to escape the RAIN and the FLOODS and the WIND!

Narrator: And so the Man went INTO his house and LOCKED the door. He listened to the WEATHER REPORTS, waiting for the STORM to arrive.

Weatherman: *(Offstage, over sound system, as if on radio)* HEY, guys and gals! Don't forget that SUN-SCREEN! CLEAR SKIES, high of 85, low of 70! And that's pretty much how it's going to STAY as far as the eye can SEE!

Man: *(From behind house)* AARRGGH! *(**Neighbor** beckons **Friends**, who go with him behind sand-based house.)*

Narrator: ONE day, however, the man heard NOISES from next DOOR. *(Sound of hammering.)*

Man: *(Peeking from behind his house)* AHA! AT LAST the storm has COME, and my NEIGHBOR'S house upon the SAND is FALLING! How GREAT will be the FALL of it! *(Man rubs his hands together.)*

(Neighbor and Friends come from behind sand-based house. Neighbor carries a hammer; Friends carry a sign that says, "COMING SOON: LUXURY BEACHFRONT RESORT." They put the sign on the sand-based house, then step back to admire their work and shake hands with each other.)

Man: *(Stepping in front of his house)* WHERE IS THAT STORM? The WISE man builds his house upon the ROCK, the FOOLISH man builds his house upon the SAND, and the RAINS come tumbling DOWN! EVERYBODY knows THAT!

(Neighbor and Friends go back behind sand-based house.)

Narrator: And behold, the rains DID come tumbling down. *(Thunder sounds. Man mimes getting rained on.)* But they tumbled ONLY on the house that had been built upon a ROCK. Not a DROP fell on the house that had been built upon the SAND.

Man: Why ME? My house may stand FIRM, but now I have to PATCH the ROOF, CLEAN the GUTTERS, and BAIL OUT the BASEMENT! What must my NEIGHBOR do? NOTHING! *(Man goes back behind his house.)*

Narrator: And so it WAS in the MONTHS and YEARS that FOLLOWED. *(Neighbor and Friends come from behind their house, carrying drinking glasses. They toast each other and mime happy conversation.)* The man who built his house upon the SAND got RICHER and RICHER, more and more SUCCESSFUL, HAPPIER and HAPPIER. *(Man comes from behind his house, puts up an umbrella, and angrily stands under it.)* The man who built his house upon a ROCK patched the ROOF, cleaned the GUTTERS, and bailed out the BASEMENT.

Man: I give UP! I've WAITED and WAITED, WATCHED the SKY, PATCHED and CLEANED and BAILED. A RECORD RAINFALL has descended on my house, and there's never been so much as a MIST on my NEIGHBOR'S! ANY fool can see that there's not going to BE any storm! *(Man stashes umbrella behind his house and pulls out a suitcase.)* If you can't BEAT 'em, JOIN 'em!

(Man goes to Neighbor and Friends, who receive him warmly and drink toasts to him. All go behind the sand-based house.)

Narrator: THAT NIGHT, of course, the RAIN DESCENDED. *(Thunder sounds.)* The FLOODS came, and the WINDS blew and beat upon BOTH of those houses. And the one that was built upon the SAND FELL. And GREAT was the FALL of it. *(**All** lie on floor and pull the sand-based house down on top of them. Crashing sounds.)* And the OTHER house fell NOT; for it was founded upon a ROCK. *(Pauses.)* Too bad NOBODY was HOME.

▶ **Related Scriptures:**
- Ecclesiastes 8:11-15
- Matthew 7:24-27
- James 1:2-12

▶ **Related Topics:**
- Suffering
- Relating to unbelievers
- Persevering in trials

Joan 'n' the Whale

Topics: Friendship; Evangelism

The Scene: A college dorm room and an airplane

The Simple Setup: Place three chairs next to each other, center stage. These can serve as the bed in **Joan**'s room as well as the airline seats for **Joan**, **Salesman**, and **Passenger**. **Joan** will need a suitcase (she can pantomime packing and unpacking the suitcase), a Bible, fish-shaped earrings and a cross necklace. (An oversized cardboard cross will add a humorous touch.) **Salesman** and **Passenger** will each need one magazine; **Skyjacker** should have a toy gun. **Salesman** should wear a suit; the rest may wear casual clothes.

The Sound: If you're using stationary microphones, set up one or two in front of the chairs. Let **Narrator** and **Voice of God** share an offstage mike, which **Joan** also uses when she's in the "belly of the plane."

Other Options: If you can find a few pith helmets (check a costume shop for the plastic foam kind), **Joan** could load them into her suitcase while packing and wear one during the airplane scene.

The Characters:

> **Narrator**, dignified but not stuffy
> **Joan**, a smug college student
> **Voice of God**, impressively booming but warm
> **Salesman**, average but excitable
> **Skyjacker**, harsh and shifty-eyed
> **Passenger**, an average person

*(As the lights come up, **Joan** is sitting on her bed reading a Bible and pantomiming eating a candy bar.)*

Narrator: When the WORD of the LORD came to JOAN, she was in her DORM ROOM eating a candy bar, LISTENING to the RADIO, and having her QUIET TIME, all at ONCE. Out of RESPECT for the STILL, SMALL VOICE, she stopped CHEWING and turned the RADIO DOWN a little.

God: *(Offstage, through sound system)* JOAN...

Narrator: Said GOD...

God: I want you to ARISE and go across the HALL to MIN NINIVER, the girl who lives in room 207. And I want you to be her FRIEND.

Narrator: Joan CHUCKLED. *(**Joan** chuckles.)* Then she GIGGLED. *(**Joan** giggles.)* Then she laughed so hard that her FISH-SHAPED EARRINGS and her CROSS NECKLACE shook. *(**Joan** laughs loudly, then finally calms down.)*

Joan: *(Chuckling)* Come ON, God…

Narrator: She said…

Joan: DON'T kid ME. I'm a BUSY PERSON. You know PERFECTLY WELL I've got to STUDY HARD so I can be a MISSIONARY for you in UPPER TARSHISHSTAN!

God: JOAN…

Narrator: Said GOD, not sounding AMUSED…

God: I am NOT KIDDING.

Narrator: Joan CLOSED her BIBLES…FIVE VERSIONS, not counting the PARAPHRASE…and FROWNED in EXASPERATION at the CEILING.

Joan: LORD…

Narrator: She said…

Joan: That's simply OUT OF THE QUESTION. MIN NINIVER'S the girl they call "The WHALE." She must weigh 300 POUNDS. If I were SEEN with her, I'd be a SOCIAL OUTCAST. And that would just RUIN my WITNESS!

(She looks up as if expecting a reply, but there is only silence.)

Narrator: Joan looked at the CEILING again, but saw only the LIGHT FIXTURE. To her SUR-PRISE, God did not REPEAT himself. *(Joan shrugs and goes back to studying.)* In FACT, he did not repeat himself for the next SIX MONTHS. Not that Joan WORRIED about it; she was BUSY those days. *(Joan starts packing a suitcase.)* Before she KNEW it, she was ready to FLY AWAY to UPPER TARSHISHSTAN. So she packed her SUITCASE full of PITH HELMETS and boarded a PLANE to the FARAWAY LAND.

*(Joan sits, facing audience, smiling and clutching her suitcase. She is joined by **Salesman** and **Passenger**, who sit next to her and read magazines. **Joan** settles in, yawns, and falls asleep.)*

Narrator: Unknown to JOAN, however, the Lord had sent a SKYJACKER onto her flight. *(Enter Skyjacker, brandishing gun.)* Halfway across the ATLANTIC OCEAN, he pulled out his GUNS and HAND GRENADES.

Skyjacker: NOBODY MOVE! I'm takin' this plane to…IOWA! *(Skyjacker strikes a pose, pointing the gun in the air and keeping a wary eye on the others.)*

Narrator: And EVERYONE was SORE AFRAID. (*Salesman* and *Passenger* panic.) But not JOAN. She was sound ASLEEP in her seat, next to a nervous HARDWARE SALESMAN from TRENTON, NEW JERSEY.

Salesman: (*Shaking* Joan) Wake UP! How can you SLEEP through this? We're being SKYJACKED!

Joan: HUH? WHAT?

Salesman: I notice that you wear a CROSS. Maybe if you PRAY, we'll get OUT of this mess!

Joan: I'm glad you SUGGESTED that! (*She whips a Bible out of her suitcase.*) Allow me to WITNESS to you!

(*Joan pantomimes nonstop reading of verses to* **Salesman** *and* **Passenger** *as the* **Narrator** *speaks.* **Skyjacker** *exits.*)

Narrator: And Joan proceeded to read THIRTY-FOUR BIBLE VERSES to the hardware Salesman, as well as presenting a SYSTEMATIC THEOLOGY to the REST of the Passengers, including a SENATOR, two ARMY GENERALS, a BASEBALL PLAYER, and several MINISTERS. (*Salesman* and *Passenger, looking miserable, sink lower in their chairs as* **Joan** *keeps up her pantomime.*) And it came to PASS that a SKYJACKER burst into the cabin. (*Skyjacker enters.*)

Skyjacker: All RIGHT! I want one HOSTAGE to stay with US. We're going to let the REST of you GO!

Salesman and
Passenger: (*In unison, pointing at* **Joan**) Take HER! (*Skyjacker takes* **Joan** *by the arm and pulls her toward the exit. All the while, she keeps up her verse-reading pantomime.*)

Salesman and
Passenger: (*Unison*) THANK YOU! (*Skyjacker exits with* **Joan** *in tow.* **Salesman** *and* **Passenger** *exit opposite.*)

Narrator: Soon the plane LANDED. The PASSENGERS were set FREE. But JOAN was TIED UP in the CARGO HOLD. And she was in the BELLY OF THE PLANE for THREE DAYS and THREE NIGHTS. (*Pauses.*) FINALLY Joan PRAYED to the LORD from the BELLY OF THE PLANE, saying…

Joan: (*From offstage, through sound system*) Very WELL, Lord. If you get me OUT of here, I will return and WITNESS to the WHALE—I mean, to MIN.

God: Just a MOMENT…

Narrator: God said…

God: I said nothing about WITNESSING. I only said "FRIEND."

Joan: RIGHT...

Narrator: Joan said. *(Pauses.)* And the Lord SPOKE to the SKYJACKER, and he KICKED Joan OUT upon the LANDING STRIP. *(Joan leaps back onstage as if kicked, landing on the floor. She picks herself up and dusts herself off.)* Soon Joan RETURNED to her DORM ROOM. *(She goes to chairs and unpacks suitcase as Narrator speaks.)* A few months LATER she was MIN NINIVER's friend. After much LABOR, lo and behold, Joan introduced Min to her OTHER friend, GOD. And the THREE of them became BETTER FRIENDS than ever. *(Pauses.)* Then ONE DAY the WORD of the LORD came to Joan a SECOND time, saying...

God: Joan, ARISE!

Joan: Oh, NO! Where to THIS time?

God: Why, to UPPER TARSHISHSTAN, of course.

Joan: AHH...

Narrator: Said Joan. *(Pauses.)* THIS time she took a BOAT.

(Joan exits.)

▶ **Related Scriptures:**
- Jonah 1–3
- Titus 2:9–10
- 1 Peter 3:13–17

▶ **Related Topics:**
- Relating to unbelievers
- God's guidance
- Missions

Junk Mail

Topic: Stewardship

The Scene: A couple's living room

The Simple Setup: Place a table and two chairs center stage. You'll also need a stack of mail containing at least nine sealed envelopes with sheets of paper in them.

The Sound: If you're using stationary microphones, put one or two on the table.

Other Options: If you want to emphasize the cartoonish nature of the characters, you might dress them in outfits such as a big bow tie for **Man**, a polka-dot dress for **Woman**, and bright colors for both.

The Characters:

    Woman, empty-headed and self-absorbed

    Man, just like his wife

▲ ▲ ▲ ▲ ▲ ▲ ▲ ▲

*(As the skit begins, **Man** sits at a table. **Woman** enters, carrying stack of mail.)*

Woman: OOH! Look at all the MAIL we got!

Man: Yeah, but I bet a LOT of it is...

Woman: Right...

Unison: JUNK mail! *(**Woman** dumps mail on table.)*

Man: OK, let's SORT it OUT. KEEPERS in THIS pile, JUNK MAIL in THIS pile.

Woman: *(Handing him an envelope)* THIS one's addressed to YOU.

Man: *(Opening envelope)* HEY, it's an ADVERTISEMENT! For just $29.95, we can get these great ADDRESS LABELS! And what a neat ADDRESS they have on them...MARY SMITH, ANYTOWN, U.S.A.!

Woman: What a BARGAIN!

Unison: It's a KEEPER!

Man: *(Handing her an envelope)* THIS one's for YOU.

Woman: *(Opening envelope)* Oh, it's one of those FUND-RAISING LETTERS! They want us to give $10 to help an ORPHAN in GUATEMALA.

Man: What do they think we ARE, made of MONEY?

Unison: JUNK mail!

Man: *(Handing her an envelope)* Try THIS one.

Woman: *(Opening envelope)* OOH, a CATALOG from the MEAT-OF-THE-MONTH CLUB. You can get a GIFT PACK of TWO WHOLE HOT DOGS for just $59.95! Let's get one for EVERY PERSON WE KNOW!

Man: OK!

Unison: It's a KEEPER!

Woman: *(Handing him an envelope)* Here's ANOTHER.

Man: *(Opening envelope)* Aw, another FUND-RAISING letter. This one wants $25 to send BIBLES to CHINA!

Woman: What ARE we, MILLIONAIRES?

Unison: JUNK mail!

Man: *(Picking up and opening envelope)* Oh, Boy, COUPONS! Let's see…twenty-five cents off BREADED BREAD STICKS…fifty cents off a VACATION in TAHITI…and a dollar REBATE on BRAIN SURGERY!

Woman: THOSE are all things we NEED!

Unison: It's a KEEPER!

Man: *(Handing her an envelope)* YOUR turn.

Woman: *(Opening envelope)* What IS it with these FUND-RAISING LETTERS? Listen to THIS! "Dear FRIENDS: Your DONATION of $50 will be an INVESTMENT in the KINGDOM. THINK of the SOULS who could be reached by just ONE more MISSIONARY in this VITAL REGION…BLAH, BLAH, BLAH.

Man: BLAH, BLAH, BLAH.

Unison: JUNK mail!

Woman: *(Handing him an envelope)* HERE.

Man: *(Opening envelope)* Oh, WOW! It's an application for a NEW CREDIT CARD!

Woman: Thank GOODNESS! We've CHARGED over the LIMIT on the eighty-seven cards we ALREADY have!

Man: But we NEEDED all those things! A BIGGER TV…

Woman: A bigger ENTERTAINMENT CENTER to put the TV in…

Man: A bigger ROOM to put the ENTERTAINMENT CENTER in…

Woman: A bigger HOUSE to put the ROOM in…

Man: And NOW we can charge a bigger LAWN MOWER for our bigger LAWN!

Unison: It's a KEEPER!

Man: *(Handing her an envelope)* ONE more.

Woman: *(Opening envelope)* This is RIDICULOUS! Another FUND-RAISER! Something about our CHURCH needing a NEW ROOF! JUNK!

Man: *(Looking at envelope)* No, WAIT! This one is DIFFERENT!

Woman: You mean…it's DIFFERENT because we need to feel a sense of RESPONSIBILITY for the FINANCIAL SITUATION of our own FELLOWSHIP?

Man: *(Standing)* NO! This one is different because…it's got an ELVIS STAMP on it!!

Woman: *(Standing)* An ELVIS STAMP? That's just what we need for our EXTENSIVE COLLEC-TION of ELVIS MEMORABILIA!

Man: Let's go put it in one of those 37-KARAT GOLD FRAMES we got from the HOME SHOPPING NETWORK!

Unison: It's a KEEPER!

(They exit.)

Related Scriptures:
- Malachi 3:8-10
- Matthew 6:19-34
- Luke 6:38

Related Topics:
- Giving
- Missions
- Materialism
- Priorities
- Putting God's kingdom first

Men in Gray

Topic: Joy

The Scene: A city street

The Simple Setup: No set is needed. This skit is a spoof of the movie *Men in Black*. The closer your actors can get to the spirit of the originals (Tommy Lee Jones as the deadpan agent, Will Smith as the streetwise one), the better. You'll need a suitcase containing the following props: two toy ray guns (or squirt guns that don't look like conventional weapons); two of the largest tank-bearing (but empty) squirt guns you can find (the "Super Soaker" type); a cell phone or walkie-talkie; and a small, working flash camera or strobe. **Agents A** and **B** should wear sunglasses and gray suits with white shirts and gray ties; **Alien** can wear casual clothes with a long fabric or foam rubber tail coming out of the back of his or her pants. **Bystander** should wear matronly street clothes.

The Sound: If you're using stationary microphones, set two at center stage, and if possible, two down-stage center. (If possible, the latter two should be at a lower level for use when the agents are firing at the evil invader.) Using prerecorded sound effects ("zap" or "outer space" sounds for ray guns, roaring, and explosion) are recommended. You'll also need a ringing sound such as that made by a cell phone.

Other Options: If you want to put extra time and some silver paint into making the agents' futuristic hardware look more impressive, have fun.

The Characters:
    Agent A, deadpan but intense
    Agent B, streetwise and emotional
    Alien, a humanoid obviously hiding something
    Bystander, a curious lady

*(As the lights come up, **Agents A** and **B** stand center stage with their backs to the audience. A suitcase sits nearby. As soon as the lights are up, they quickly turn to face the audience, striking a macho pose with their arms crossed in front of their chests.)*

Agent B:		*(Breaking pose)* Man, how come we gotta wear these SUITS? Haven't you got any-thing with a little PERSONALITY?
Agent A:		You don't NEED a personality anymore. You're part of…the MEN IN GRAY.
Agent B:		Yeah, I KNOW, but…
Agent A:		You DO want to be one of the MEN IN GRAY, DON'T you?
Agent B:		Well, SURE! I mean, FIGHTING ALIENS, SAVING THE EARTH, and all that…

Agent A: But it's TOP SECRET.

Agent B: RIGHT. Like the CIA.

Agent A: More secret than THAT.

Agent B: Then it's like the OPQ.

Agent A: Never HEARD of it.

Agent B: There you GO.

Agent A: You must ALWAYS address me as AGENT A. And YOU are AGENT B.

Agent B: Can't I be something a little more COLORFUL? Like Agent ORANGE?

Agent A: NO. We're the...

Agent B: MEN IN GRAY. Yeah, I KNOW. So what's our assignment TODAY?

Agent A: Watch for ALIENS. You'll need THIS. *(Opens suitcase, takes out toy ray gun, gives it to B, and takes another ray gun for self.)* SUBATOMIC PARTICLE DISRUPTER.

Agent B: WOW!

*(Enter **Alien**, who looks like a normal human except for the long tail dragging behind him or her. **Alien** keeps looking back and forth nervously.)*

Agent A: SHH! THERE'S one!

Agent B: One WHAT?

Agent A: ALIEN.

Agent B: Now, how can you tell THAT?

Agent A: Call it a HUNCH. When you've been in this business as long as I have, you just get a FEELING. *(To **Alien**)* YOU there...with the TAIL!

Alien: *(As if English is an unfamiliar language)* Are—are you INSTRUCTING to ME? Hearty GREETINGS! I am quite the NATIVE to this PLANET, you see!

Agent A: Yeah, and I'm BETSY ROSS' FLAG! Go back to that GASSY NEBULA you CAME from, pal!

Alien: *(Suddenly growling and hissing)* I will DISMANTLE you FIRST, PUNY EARTHMAN!

Agent A: *(To B)* GET him!

*(They aim their guns at **Alien**. "Zap" or "outer space" noises.)*

Alien: ARRGGH! *(Stumbles backward as if hit, falls offstage.)*

Agent B: WHOA! We GOT him! COOL!

*(**Bystander** enters, looking dismayed. She keeps glancing offstage where **Alien** fell.)*

Agent A: UH–oh.

Bystander: Oh, MY! Did you SEE that?

Agent A: Uh…see WHAT, Ma'am?

Bystander: Why, that CREATURE! It fell DOWN, and all that yellowish BLOOD started leaking out of it! *(Looks at **A** and **B**.)* Who are YOU? And what are those STRANGE-LOOKING WEAPONS?

Agent A: *(Reaching into suitcase)* Just a MOMENT, ma'am. I can explain EVERYTHING.

*(**Agent A** takes a camera-sized device from suitcase, points it at **Bystander**. A flash goes off.)*

Bystander: I…Where AM I? I must be WALKING down the STREET, MINDING my own BUSINESS.

Agent A: THAT'S right, ma'am. Have a nice DAY.

*(Dazed, **Bystander** crosses stage and exits.)*

Agent B: *(To **Agent A**)* What did you DO? *(Pointing at flash device)* What's THAT thing?

Agent A: We call it the NUMBALYZER. It WIPES OUT the MEMORY of ALIEN INCIDENTS. TOP SECRET, remember?

Agent B: Yeah. I guess that's…

*(Beeping or phone ringing sound. **Agent A** takes a cell phone or walkie-talkie from suitcase.)*

Agent A: This is A. *(Pauses.)* Yes, SIR. *(Pauses.)* I UNDERSTAND, sir. We'll get right ON it.

Agent B: What NOW?

Agent A: He's BACK. And he's headed this WAY.

Agent B: WHO?

Agent A: The most EVIL INVADER of ALL…and he's out to ENSLAVE every MAN, WOMAN, and CHILD on the PLANET.

Agent B: *(Looking around)* What does he LOOK like?

Agent A: He takes MANY forms. FIRST time he came to earth, he looked like a SNAKE. But he could look like ANYTHING…even an ANGEL OF LIGHT.

Agent B: *(Looking over heads of audience)* Uh…Agent A?

Agent A: Yeah?

Agent B: What's RED and GREEN and SLIMY and about TEN STORIES TALL?

Agent A: I give up. What's RED and GREEN and SLIMY and about TEN STORIES TALL?

Agent B: I don't KNOW…but it's standing right THERE! *(Points over heads of audience.)*

(Roaring sound.)

Agent A: It's HIM! Fire AWAY!

(They point their guns over heads of audience. "Zap" or "outer space" noises. Finally they stop shooting and stare over heads of audience.)

Agent B: It's not WORKING! *(Sound: roaring.)* What are we gonna DO? We can't let this SLIME-BALL take over the WORLD!

Agent A: It's time to bring out the BIG GUNS. *(Puts ray guns back into suitcase; takes out two huge "Super Soaker" type water guns, and gives one to **Agent B**.)*

Agent B: WOW! What are THESE?

Agent A: The BIG GUNS. *(Pauses.)* On MY SIGNAL, crank it all the way UP and FIRE!

(They go down on one knee and aim over heads of audience.)

Agent A: One…two…THREE! *(Sound: louder "zap" or "outer space" noise, which continues until further notice.)* Keep it UP!

Agent B: The weapons are OVERHEATING, man! They're gonna BLOW!

Agent A: Don't stop NOW! The FUTURE of the HUMAN RACE is at stake!

*(Sound: huge explosion. Gun sound stops. **A** and **B** lower their weapons and stand up.)*

Agent B: He's GONE! We DID it, man! The planet is SAVED!

Agent A: *(Looking at audience)* UH-oh.

Agent B: WHAT?

Agent A: *(Pointing at audience)* All those PEOPLE out there. They saw the whole THING.

Agent B: So WHAT, man? Now they can PARTY! They've been SAVED! SAVED from the most EVIL INVADER in HISTORY, who wanted to turn them into SLAVES!

Agent A: We'll have to use the NUMBALYZER. *(Picks up the flash device.)*

Agent B: No WAY, man! If you use THAT, they won't remember how CLOSE they came to DISASTER! They won't know how much they have to CELEBRATE! They'll act like all this never HAPPENED!

Agent A: SORRY, B. It's POLICY. *(Aims flash device at audience.)*

Agent B: You can't DO this! They'll FORGET they've been RESCUED! They'll…

*(**Agent A** flashes the flash at the audience.)*

Agent A: OK, folks. Nothing to REJOICE about here. Just go on about your BUSINESS.

Agent B: ALL RIGHT, man. But SOMEBODY'S bound to REMEMBER! In a crowd THIS big, SOMEBODY'S going to remember. The WORD is going to get AROUND. Before you KNOW it, these people will be so PUMPED you won't be able to keep a LID on this place! You wait and SEE! You just…

*(**Agent A** flashes the flash device at **Agent B**.)*

Agent B: *(Dazed)* HUH? What's THAT? *(To **Agent A**)* Man, how come we gotta wear these SUITS? Haven't you got anything with a little PERSONALITY?

Agent A: Works every TIME.

(The lights go out.)

Related Scriptures:
- Psalm 51:12
- Psalm 126
- Galatians 4:12-15

Related Topics:
- What it means to be a Christian
- Expression in worship
- The work of Christ

The New Ump

Topic: Moral Standards

The Scene: A baseball diamond

The Simple Setup: No set is needed except for "home plate," which can be real or made of cardboard or wood. If possible, costume your actors with uniforms for the players and coaches and protective pad and mask for **Umpire** and **Catcher**. If you can't find uniforms, assume it's a sandlot game and costume accordingly. For props you'll need a whisk broom for **Umpire**, a bat for **Batter**, a mitt for **Catcher**, and a pamphlet (rulebook) for **Coach A**.

The Sound: If you're using stationary microphones, place one at home plate, one a few feet to the left of home plate, and one a few feet to the right. Use recorded sound effects for the ball hitting the mitt and the bat hitting the ball, or create these at an offstage mike.

Other Options: If your **Coaches** have the word "Coach" emblazoned on their shirts, they will be readily identified. Recorded crowd noise in the background, kept low as not to interfere with dialogue, will add depth to the scene.

The Characters:

    Umpire, a wishy-washy intellectual, condescending one moment, whiny the next
    Coach A, reasonable but easily riled
    Coach B, much like **Coach A**
    Batter, the strong, silent type
    Catcher, a no-nonsense guy

*(As the skit begins, the **Umpire** is dusting home plate with a whisk broom.)*

Umpire: *(Singing)* TAKE me out to the BALL GAME…

*(**Coach A** enters.)*

Coach A: HEY! Who are YOU?

Umpire: Why, I'm the NEW UMPIRE.

Coach A: What happened to the OLD one?

Umpire: There was…shall we say…a SUBSTITUTION.

Coach A: WHAT? The OLD ump was doing a GREAT job. He's ALWAYS done a great job!

Umpire: YES, yes, I understand. It's NATURAL to RESIST CHANGE. But in TIME you'll come to see that the NEW ways are BEST.

Coach A: But...

Umpire: PLAY BALL!

(**Coach A** mutters under his breath, walks to the side of the stage, and stands there with his arms crossed. **Batter** and **Catcher** enter and take their positions at the plate. **Umpire** stands behind **Catcher** in the typical fashion. **Batter** warms up, takes his stance, and watches an imaginary ball whiz past and into the mitt of the **Catcher**.)

(Sound of ball hitting mitt. **Catcher** takes imaginary ball from mitt and throws it back to imaginary pitcher—toward audience. **All** look at **Umpire** as if expecting him to say something.)

Batter: SO? Was it a STRIKE or a BALL?

Umpire: (Scratching his chin) Well, that DEPENDS. I'd hate to set myself up as a JUDGE, after all.

Coach B: (Entering) WAIT a minute! Are you saying you can't DECIDE whether that was a BALL or a STRIKE? The OLD ump ALWAYS knew!

Umpire: AH, yes. That's PRECISELY why he had to GO. He was HOPELESSLY out of DATE, always IMPOSING his VALUE JUDGMENTS on OTHERS. IMAGINE...acting as though everything were CUT and DRIED...a STRIKE or a BALL...a SAFE or an OUT!

Coach A: Yeah. Imagine THAT.

Umpire: We know NOW, of course, that these are GRAY areas. One man's SAFE is another man's OUT.

Batter: So what do we CALL it?

Umpire: Um...A STRIKEBALL.

Others: (Unison) A STRIKEBALL?

Umpire: YES. Now, let's go on with the GAME...please.

(Shaking their heads, the others take their positions. **Batter** warms up, takes his stance, and swings at imaginary ball.)

(Sound of bat hitting ball. **Batter** drops bat and exits as though running to first base.)

Coach B: A BASE HIT!

Coach A: No WAY! It's a FOUL!

Coach B: FAIR!

Coach A: FOUL!

Coach B: FAIR!

Coach A: FOUL!

Umpire: Gentlemen, GENTLEMEN! It's a FOULFAIR!

Coaches A and B: *(Unison)* WHAT?

Umpire: A FOULFAIR. Who's to say what's FOUL and what ISN'T? I certainly can't. The COURTS can't come up with a definition. In SOME cultures, what's FOUL is FAIR and what's FAIR is…

Coach A: I know a foul when I SEE it!

Coach B: So do I!

Umpire: NOW, now. You're being SUBJECTIVE. ONE person's view is as good as ANOTHER'S.

Coach A: HOLD it. *(He pulls a pamphlet from his back pocket.)* Here's the RULE BOOK. We've ALWAYS gone by the RULE BOOK.

Umpire: Yes, I KNOW. NOBODY believes that old thing anymore. It's filled with MISTAKES!

Coach B: It IS?

Umpire: For ONE thing, it doesn't tell how BASEBALLS are MANUFACTURED…which proves it's UNSCIENTIFIC. For ANOTHER thing, it's been around since ABNER DOUBLEDAY. Who KNOWS how many ERRORS have been added as it's been handed DOWN?

Coach A: WOW, I never THOUGHT of it that way before!

Coach B: But if the RULE BOOK is no good, how can we come up with a way to play the GAME?

Umpire: Why, we'll just VOTE! Any time we need a RULE, we'll ask the FANS. We'll GO ALONG WITH THE CROWD! *(To audience)* LADIES AND GENTLEMEN, how many of you feel that was a FOUL BALL? Please indicate by CLAPPING YOUR HANDS. *(Pauses.)* How many of you feel it was FAIR?

Coach A: I KNEW they'd see it MY way!

Coach B: What are you TALKING about? They were on MY side!

Coach A: Oh, so you're DEAF as well as BLIND!

Coach B: Why, YOU…

(Coaches start strangling each other, which they continue to do for the rest of the skit, even when they're talking.)

Catcher: I QUIT! What's the point of playing with no RULES? *(He throws down his mitt and exits.)*

Coach A: All RIGHT! There's only ONE WAY to RESOLVE this!

Coach B: We've got to get the OLD UMP back!

Coach A: On SECOND thought, if the OLD ump saw us NOW…

Coach B: He'd probably throw us BOTH out of the STADIUM for ACTING this way!

Coach A: So FORGET THAT!

Coach B: YEAH! *(Coaches wrestle each other to the ground, where they continue to fight.)*

Umpire: *(After a pause)* Um…PLAY BALL? *(Pauses.)* YOO hoo! ANYONE? Oh, dear ME. Can't we all just GET ALONG?

▶ **Related Scriptures:**
- Exodus 20:1-17
- Nehemiah 9:13-38
- Proverbs 14:12

▶ **Related Topics:**
- Relativism
- The authority of Scripture
- Tolerance

The Conversion of Paul Bunyan

Topic: Accepting One Another

The Scene: A street corner

The Simple Setup: No set is needed. **Businessman** should be dressed in suit and overcoat and carry a briefcase; **Little Man** is dressed shabbily. (Include a stocking cap if possible.) **Little Man** need not be unusually short, but should be shorter than **Businessman**.

The Sound: If you're using stationary microphones, put two at center stage.

Other Options: To give **Little Man** an unshaven look, apply a bit of dark mascara or greasepaint where his beard stubble would be.

The Characters:
    Businessman, in a hurry
    Little Man, a timid, wistful, homeless person

*(As the skit begins, **Businessman** stands center stage. He looks at his watch.)*

Businessman: Where IS that BUS?

*(Enter **Little Man**, unshaven and dressed shabbily. He glances around furtively, a haunted look in his eyes. Finally he steps hesitantly toward the **Businessman**, taking off his stocking cap and twisting it in his hands.)*

Little Man: EXCUSE me...

*(**Businessman** looks at **Little Man** and steps back uncomfortably.)*

Businessman: I–I'm SORRY. I haven't GOT any CASH. *(He looks at his watch again.)*

Little Man: Oh, THAT'S all right, sir.

Businessman: *(After a pause)* SO, what do you WANT?

Little Man: *(Grabbing sleeve of **Businessman**)* Have—have you seen BABE?

Businessman: *(Pulling away)* WHO?

Little Man: BABE!

Businessman: LOOK, I…uh…Maybe you should go SLEEP IT OFF.

Little Man: Oh, I haven't been DRINKING, sir. *(He looks down, embarrassed.)* I was not ALWAYS as you see me NOW.

Businessman: Uh-huh. You used to be RICH, right?

Little Man: NO, no…I used to be TALLER!

Businessman: You don't SAY.

Little Man: Perhaps you've HEARD of me. My name is…PAUL BUNYAN.

Businessman: NOPE. SORRY. The only PAUL BUNYAN I ever heard of was in those FOLK TALES we read in GRADE SCHOOL!

Little Man: YES, YES! A GIANT LOGGER from the NORTH WOODS. He leveled whole FORESTS with one stroke of his AX. He had a BIG, BLUE OX named BABE!

Businessman: *(Checking his watch)* RIGHT.

Little Man: That's ME! I'm PAUL BUNYAN!

Businessman: Um…the Paul Bunyan I'm talking about was a lot TALLER!

Little Man: I KNOW. *(He stares wistfully into the distance.)* I was SO BIG that when I WALKED, LAKES formed in my FOOTPRINTS. I ate FLAPJACKS so HUGE that the COOKS greased the GRIDDLE by SKATING on slabs of BACON. I had a LAUGH so HEARTY it could be heard from ONE end of the woods to…

Businessman: YEAH, that's the ONE. But PAUL BUNYAN'S just a TALL TALE…a FOLK hero. He's not REAL!

Little Man: Do I LOOK like a FOLK HERO?

Businessman: No. But PAUL BUNYAN was tall enough to touch the TOPS of the TREES. YOU'RE so…SHORT!

Little Man: *(Lowering his head)* I KNOW. That's because I got…CONVERTED!

Businessman: CONVERTED?

Little Man: *(Staring straight ahead)* Yes! ONE SUNDAY MORNING about a YEAR ago, BABE and I left the NORTH WOODS. We WALKED until we found a CHURCH. I KNOCKED on the ROOF, and they sent out some MEN to talk to me. They wouldn't let me WALK THE AISLE...said it wasn't WIDE ENOUGH. But THAT was the day I got CONVERTED.

Businessman: Really.

Little Man: They BAPTIZED me in the nearest LAKE. I was so TALL I FLOODED THE BANKS. FISH were stacked TEN FEET DEEP around the SHORE when I got OUT.

Businessman: Right.

Little Man: The CHURCH BUILDING wasn't BIG enough for me, of course. So BABE and I would sit on a HILL next to the church, listening to the SERMON over a LOUDSPEAKER. I didn't KNOW the HYMNS, but I'd do my BEST to sing ALONG. *(He sighs.)* THAT'S... when it STARTED.

Businessman: WHAT started?

Little Man: FIRST the CHURCH PEOPLE told me I was singing PRAISES too LOUDLY. It made the PEWS vibrate, they said. So I had to STOP SINGING and just HUM.

Businessman: I SEE. *(To himself)* Where IS that BUS?

Little Man: THEN they told me that if I was TRULY converted, I couldn't DRESS like a LUMBER-JACK. They made me get RID of my PLAID SHIRT, my SUSPENDERS, my OVERALLS, my BOOTS. I had to wear...a BLUE POLYESTER SUIT instead. *(He looks down.)* THAT'S when...I NOTICED it.

Businessman: Noticed WHAT?

Little Man: That I wasn't quite as TALL as I used to be. It wasn't MUCH of a difference...just a few FEET. So I FORGOT about it...until...

Businessman: Until WHAT?

Little Man: Until they made me STAY OUT OF THE WOODS. They said CONVERTED people shouldn't hang around with those ROUGH types...like LUMBERJACKS.

Businessman: But YOU were a lumberjack!

Little Man: Not ANYMORE. They told me I couldn't TALK or LAUGH or SMELL like a lumberjack now that I was CONVERTED. I had to stop yelling "TIMBER" and start saying "AMEN." I had to SHAVE MY BEARD and stop ROAMING THE WOODS with BABE. They made me take a job as an INSURANCE SALESMAN and moved me to the SUBURBS.

Businessman: (Checking his watch) But how could you LIVE there? Weren't you TOO BIG?

Little Man: (Shaking his head) Every time I did something to FIT IN with the CHURCH PEOPLE, I got SMALLER. Finally I was down to THEIR level. THEY seemed pleased, but I didn't feel like MYSELF anymore.

Businessman: Do you expect me to believe that getting CONVERTED made you SHORTER?

Little Man: Oh, NO…it wasn't the CONVERSION. It was having to BE LIKE THE OTHERS! I had to SHRINK to FIT!

Businessman: (Throwing up his hands) LOOK, Mr. Bunyan—or whatever your REAL name is—people don't end up on SKID ROW just because they're SHORT. What are YOU doing here?

Little Man: (His lip trembling) They—they SENT BABE AWAY. They told me BLUE OXEN just didn't fit into their THEOLOGY. I've been WANDERING the COUNTRY ever SINCE, looking for my OLD COMPANION. (He wipes away a tear.)

(**Businessman** rolls his eyes and shakes his head. He checks his watch again.)

Businessman: Well…that sure is a SAD STORY, Mr.…BUNYAN. But I'm LATE for an APPOINTMENT. You just keep looking for that GIANT BLUE OX, and I'm sure you'll FIND him…or HER.

Little Man: (Nodding resignedly and putting his cap back on) THANK you. THANK you, sir.

(**Little Man** exits.)

Businessman: (To himself) MAN! What a NUT! All that nonsense about SHRINKING TO FIT IN! (Glancing around) Good thing nobody SAW me. I can't be seen talking to somebody like THAT! I mean, what would the people from CHURCH think?

(**Businessman** exits.)

▶ **Related Scriptures:**
- Matthew 7:1-5
- Romans 15:1-7
- Galatians 5:1-15

▶ **Related Topics:**
- Legalism
- Relating to unbelievers
- What it means to be a Christian

Return of the Living Dead

Topic: Following Jesus

The Scene: A tomb

The Simple Setup: You'll need a long, sturdy table (center stage) and a white sheet for wrapping **Lazarus**. Try to make the stage as dark as you can, except for a light on **Lazarus**.

The Sound: If you're using stationary microphones, put one next to the table for **Lazarus**. An offstage mike should be used for the voice of **Jesus**.

Other Options: If you like, you can add the sound effect of a large rock being moved at the end of the skit, as indicated by the dialogue.

The Characters:

    Lazarus, formerly dead; now lazy and irritable
    Jesus, authoritative voice heard from offstage

*(As the skit begins, the stage is as dark as possible, except where **Lazarus** lies on a table. He is wrapped in a white sheet, with only his head exposed.)*

Jesus: *(Offstage throughout, over sound system)* Lazarus, come forth!

Lazarus: Huh? What? HEY! I thought I was…SLEEPING. How come my MATTRESS is so HARD? Feels like a— Well, what do you KNOW? It IS a rock. What am I doing lying on a ROCK? And how come it's so DARK in here? What's this CLOTH I'm wrapped in? It's almost like I was—oh, that's RIGHT. I WAS dead. *(Pauses.)* DEAD? Well, then, how can I be…

Jesus: Lazarus, come FORTH!

Lazarus: *(Sitting up)* What's all the NOISE? It's loud enough to raise the…Oh. Somebody's YELLING at me. Now why would anybody yell at a DEAD person? Can't I get any PEACE and QUIET ANYWHERE?

Jesus: Lazarus, COME FORTH!

Lazarus: WAIT a minute. I RECOGNIZE that voice. What's HE doing here? Where was he when I NEEDED him? Probably off somewhere HEALING the LEPERS and making the LAME WALK and the BLIND SEE. And all the while I was DYING. NOW he shows up. What PERFECT TIMING!

Jesus: Lazarus, COME FORTH!

Lazarus: He wants me to come OUT? What is he, CRAZY? DEAD people don't come out of their TOMBS. Especially not after THREE DAYS! Where does he think they got that saying, "REST IN PEACE"? Doesn't he have any RESPECT for the DEAD? *(He looks around then down at himself.)* HEY! Is it my IMAGINATION, or am I SITTING UP? Since when do DEAD people sit UP?

Jesus: LAZARUS, come FORTH!

Lazarus: What's going ON here? WHAT am I…ALIVE? Oh, GREAT! Here I was, NICE and DEAD, MINDING my own BUSINESS…and all of a sudden I have to come back to LIFE! Whose idea WAS this?

Jesus: LAZARUS, come FORTH!

Lazarus: I should have KNOWN! This is JUST the sort of thing he'd do. He's always telling people, "FOLLOW ME," or "SELL ALL YOU HAVE AND GIVE TO THE POOR," or "GO AND SIN NO MORE." Always CALLING and CHANGING and SENDING, never leaving well enough ALONE! Did he ASK me whether I wanted to come back from the dead? NOOO! Did he think for a moment of MY comfort and well-being? Of COURSE not!

Jesus: Lazarus, COME FORTH!

Lazarus: I suppose he thinks it's so GREAT out there that I should JUMP at the chance to come out. But he just doesn't realize how NICE it is in here. It's so QUIET—or at least it was before he started SHOUTING! And I like the DÉCOR…SIMPLE, with lots of EARTH TONES. No BAD WEATHER, no SUNBURN, no worries about what MARTHA might cook for DINNER…

Jesus: Lazarus, COME FORTH!

Lazarus: And no having to decide every day what I'll WEAR. These WRAPPINGS are a little TIGHT, but then who needs MOBILITY if you're not GOING anywhere? There's a certain COMFORT in always knowing where you'll BE. And it's so SAFE here. Or at least it WOULD be if they'd roll that STONE back where it's SUPPOSED to be!

Jesus: LAZARUS, come FORTH!

Lazarus: What's this "COME FORTH" business? What does he WANT from me, anyway? I'll bet the MINUTE I step out of here, he'll ask me to DO something for him. Well, he can forget THAT! THIS is where I belong, right here with my COMFORTABLE SLAB and GRAVE CLOTHS, like any NORMAL person!

Jesus: Lazarus...

(There is a long pause.)

Lazarus: Well, it's about TIME! He's finally given UP! Sure TOOK him long enough. *(Pauses.)* What's that NOISE? Ah, they're finally rolling the STONE back into place! Now maybe I can get some REST! *(He lies down.)* Wow, it really IS dark in here. And QUIET...REAL quiet. And COOL, and...and...*(Pauses.)* SAY...what's that awful SMELL?

(The stage goes dark.)

▶ **Related Scriptures:**
- Luke 9:23
- John 11:1-44
- Romans 6:1-14

▶ **Related Topics:**
- The abundant life
- Taking up your cross
- Leaving the past behind

The Parable of the Talents

Topic: Spiritual Gifts

The Scene: An estate with many servants

The Simple Setup: No set is needed. If you use contemporary costumes, dress the **Master** in a suit and the **Servants** in work clothes.

The Sound: If you're using stationary microphones, place three of them at equal intervals across the stage. Plan the action so that your actors will be near one of them to deliver their lines. The **Narrator** will need an offstage mike.

Other Options: Medieval costumes (peasant dress for **Servants** and finery for **Master**) will add depth.

The Characters:

      Narrator, earnest, as if telling a classic folk tale
      Master, dignified but not pompous
      Servant One, high-energy but self-absorbed
      Servant Two, much like **Servant One**
      Servant Three, much like **Servant Two**

*(As the skit begins, **Servants** pantomime raking the ground as the **Master** mimes making notes on an imaginary tablet.)*

Narrator:	🙂	*(Offstage throughout)* And it CAME to PASS that a MAN had many SERVANTS.
Master:	🙂	My SERVANTS, gather ROUND! *(Servants gather around Master.)* I am about to EMBARK upon a long JOURNEY!
Servants:	😮	*(Unison)* OOH! A LONG JOURNEY!
Master:	🙂	While I am GONE, you must CONTINUE the WORK we have begun. To DO this, you will need…TALENTS!
Servants:	😮	*(Unison)* OOH! TALENTS!
Master:	🙂	To some I give ONE talent; to some, TWO; to others, THREE. And so EACH of you will be…TALENTED!
Servants:	😮	*(Unison)* OOH! TALENTED!
Master:	🙂	My servants, INVEST WISELY the TALENTS I have given you!

Servant One: Three CHEERS for the MASTER! Hip, hip...

Servants: *(Unison)* HOORAY!

Servant One: Hip, hip...

Servants: *(Unison)* HOORAY!

Servant One: Hip, hip...

Servants: *(Unison)* HOORAY!

*(**Master** exits, waving goodbye.)*

Servant One: Have a nice TRIP!

Servant Two: We won't let you DOWN!

Servant Three: And THANKS for the TALENTS!

*(**Servants** return to work. As **Narrator** speaks, **Servant One** tills the soil; **Servant Three** brings an imaginary cup of water to **Servant One**, who drinks it; **Servant Two** mimes talking to the others, who listen with interest.)*

Narrator: And so the servants USED their TALENTS to do the Master's WORK. Some tended the ORCHARDS...some cared for servants who were OLD or ILL...some brought WATER to those who TILLED the GROUND...and some told OTHERS of the Master's GOODNESS. People came from MILES AROUND to HEAR of the Master and join his WORK. But ONE DAY something CHANGED. *(**Servant Three** exits.)*

Servant One: *(To **Servant Two**)* SO, what talent did YOU get?

Servant Two: MENDING SHOES! That's for NOBODIES. I want to do something IMPORTANT, like getting up in FRONT at the MEETING HOUSE and SINGING about the Master!

Servant One: But mending SHOES is IMPORTANT! Wouldn't it be HARD to do the Master's work in BARE FEET?

Servant Two: So WHAT? We're talking about my FULFILLMENT here! Besides, those singers we've got NOW aren't so TALENTED, if you know what I MEAN!

Narrator: And so the servant whose talent was mending SHOES stopped USING that talent. Soon the OTHER servants' shoes started to LEAK, and they became discontented TOO. *(**Servant Three** enters.)*

Servant Three: I'm TIRED of working with WET FEET! Let's hire a SHOEMAKER!

Servant One: I want a more important job TOO! Placing LONG-DISTANCE PHONE CALLS to the Master is BORING!

Servant Two: And I'm TIRED of INVITING STRANGERS into my HOME. They EAT too much! Let somebody ELSE do it!

*(Servants mime complaining and arguing as **Narrator** speaks.)*

Narrator: Soon the LENGTH and BREADTH of the Master's property was in an UPROAR. SOME servants refused to USE their talents, while OTHERS demanded more RECOGNITION. Still OTHERS declared that certain talents should not be EXER- CISED and that the Master had not really meant to GIVE them. Finally the Master's business GROUND TO A HALT.

*(**Servant One** gets the attention of the others.)*

Servant One: MY FELLOW SERVANTS! Having received the talent of ORGANIZATION, I have called this EMERGENCY MEETING. It is CLEAR that the MASTER'S PLAN has FAILED. We cannot carry out his WORK with the TALENTS he has GIVEN us. THEREFORE, I pro- pose that we make the following CHANGES. Number ONE: Those who SPEAK THE MASTER'S WORDS AT THE MEETING HOUSE *(points at **Servant Two**)* will now take on OUR duties as well… visiting the SICK, telling OUTSIDERS about the Master, greeting STRANGERS, shaking our HANDS as we LEAVE, et cetera, et cetera, et cetera.

Servant Three: HEAR, HEAR! *(**Servant Two** slumps and groans.)*

Servant One: Number TWO: Those who SPEAK THE MASTER'S WORDS can try to CONVINCE the REST of us to USE our talents. But if they DON'T… it's… PARTY TIME!

Servant Three: Hip, hip, HOORAY! *(**Servant Two** slumps and groans. As the **Narrator** speaks, **Servants One** and **Three** stand around smiling and pretending to polish their fingernails. **Servant Two** mimes pleading with them, to no avail. Finally **Servant Two** gives up.)*

Narrator: The NEW PLAN was immensely POPULAR, at least among those who did not SPEAK the Master's WORDS. But before LONG the ORCHARDS stopped bearing quite so much FRUIT. WEEDS grew around the MEETING HOUSE, and ATTENDANCE dwindled. FEWER STRANGERS heard about the Master and his GOODNESS, and the SERVANTS got used to walking in LEAKY SHOES. SOME servants continued at their tasks, often having to PRETEND they possessed the talents of OTHERS. But MOST put their talents to DIFFERENT uses.

Servant One: *(To audience)* I have the talent of WELCOMING STRANGERS. But THAT'S no fun. I know! I'll use my talent to throw BARBECUES for my FRIENDS! *(Mimes tossing burgers on grill.)*

Servant Two: *(To audience)* I have the talent of VISITING THE SICK. But that makes me…UN-COMFORTABLE. I know! I'll use my talent to visit…faraway THEME PARKS on VACATION! *(Mimes taking pictures with imaginary camcorder.)*

Servant Three: *(To audience)* I have the talent of SINGING ABOUT THE MASTER. But that takes so much TIME. I know! I'll collect the recordings of OTHERS who'll sing FOR me! *(Mimes listening to music on headphones.)*

Narrator: The WEEDS grew LONGER…and the HARVEST grew SMALLER every YEAR. *(Master enters from rear of sanctuary and makes his way to the stage as Narrator speaks.)* FINALLY the Master RETURNED from his JOURNEY…and found only a FEW servants still at their POSTS. The SPEAKER OF THE MASTER'S WORDS was EXHAUSTED from OVERWORK, and the HARVEST filled only a TENTH of the bushel baskets it had filled in the OLD days.

Master: *(His back to audience)* My SERVANTS! What happened to the TALENTS I entrusted to you? *(Servants, surprised, stop their burger flipping, picture taking, and music listening.)*

Servant One: Uh…

Servant Two: We…

Servant Three: We BURIED them.

Narrator: And you should have seen the Master's FACE.

(The lights go out.)

▶ **Related Scriptures:**
- Matthew 25:14-30
- 1 Corinthians 12
- 1 Peter 4:7-11

▶ **Related Topics:**
- Volunteering
- Respecting church leaders
- Unity in the body

The Call

Topic: Knowing God's Will

The Scene: A sidewalk cafe

The Simple Setup: Place a small table center stage, a chair next to it, and a telephone on the table. **Stander** could wear any casual clothes; **Sitter**'s outfit (tropical print shirt, sunglasses, Bermuda shorts or jeans) and lazy pace should suggest a perpetual vacationer. **Stander**'s dashes can be off-stage or down the sanctuary aisle, whichever is more convenient. **Sitter** will need a book as a prop; cover the title so that **Sitter**'s line about studying first aid won't be given away or contradicted.

The Sound: If you're using stationary microphones, place one on a short stand next to **Sitter**; place a full-height mike nearby for **Stander**. You'll need a phone-ringing sound effect, too.

Other Options: If you want to add depth, add an umbrella-shaded table.

The Characters:
> **Sitter**, seemingly unconcerned by anything going on around him or her
> **Stander**, concerned and energetic

*(As the play begins, **Sitter** is sitting near the table, reading a book. After a few moments, **Stander** enters.)*

Stander: HEY, what do you KNOW? Is that really YOU? Long time no SEE!

Sitter: *(Yawning and looking up)* WELL, well. How long has it BEEN, anyway?

Stander: WOW, I don't KNOW. What have you been DOING all this time?

Sitter: *(Going back to reading)* STUDYING, of course.

Stander: STUDYING? Well, I guess that's…*(Squinting at something in the distance)* HEY! What's going on over THERE?

Sitter: *(Still reading)* Hmm?

Stander: An OLD MAN just fell down in the STREET. Come ON! We'd better go HELP him! *(**Stander** runs off, but **Sitter** stays put, reading. After a few moments **Stander** returns, out of breath.)* Well, HE'S okay. *(To **Sitter**)* HEY, how come you didn't give me a HAND?

Sitter: *(Looking up from book)* Why…because I'm WAITING, of course!

Stander: *(face)* Waiting for WHAT?

Sitter: *(face)* *(Nodding at phone)* For the CALL.

Stander: *(face)* What?

Sitter: *(face)* *(Pointing at phone)* The CALL!

Stander: *(face)* What is…*(Sees something else in the distance.)* *(face)* Aw, LOOK at THAT! That KID just snatched a lady's PURSE. Come ON…we can probably CATCH him! *(Stander runs off, but Sitter just sits. Soon Stander returns, huffing and puffing.)* What kind of neighborhood IS this? People FALLING in the STREET, KIDS stealing PURSES. *(face)* HEY, what's the MATTER with you? Why didn't you come WITH me?

Sitter: *(face)* *(Looking up from book)* Because I didn't get the CALL!

Stander: *(face)* WHAT call?

Sitter: *(face)* *(Glancing heavenward)* THE CALL!

Stander: *(face)* THE Call? WHAT in the…*(seeing something else in the distance)* *(face)* OOH! Did you SEE that? That CAR just took a LEFT and plowed right into the MOTORCYCLE! *(face)* Now, come ON! Don't just SIT there. We've got to HELP!

Sitter: *(face)* I'm SORRY. I'm not CALLED.

Stander: *(face)* *(As he runs off)* What are you STUDYING, anyway?

Sitter: *(face)* FIRST AID!

(Sitter goes back to reading as Stander runs out. Soon Stander returns, exhausted.)

Stander: *(face)* I've got to use your PHONE.

Sitter: *(face)* WHAT?

Stander: *(face)* I've got to call an AMBULANCE for that guy!

Sitter: *(face)* *(Wrestling Stander for the phone)* You—you can't DO that! Why, the CALL might come at any TIME! I might get the CALL any MINUTE now! *(Phone rings. Sitter and Stander freeze, surprised. Finally Sitter speaks with great drama.)* *(face)* I…oh, MY! It's…it's finally HAPPENED! *(face)* Oh, what an HONOR. At last I've received…the CALL! *(Sitter picks* up phone with trembling hands.) YES? (There is a pause as **Sitter** listens. Suddenly mood of **Sitter** turns angry. **Sitter** hands phone to **Stander**.) I—I can't BELIEVE it! It's for YOU!

(**Sitter** stalks out. **Stander** accepts the phone and listens as the lights fade out.)

▶ **Related Scriptures:**
- Matthew 25:31-46
- Ephesians 4:1
- James 2:14-26

▶ **Related Topics:**
- Faith and works
- Meeting physical needs
- Compassion

The Facts

Topic: The Resurrection

The Scene: Jerusalem, approximately 30 AD

The Simple Setup: For this spoof on the classic TV show *Dragnet*, you'll need no set. The closer your **Joe** can get to the late Jack Webb's clipped, no-nonsense monotone, the better. Since the skit mixes contemporary and first-century references, try doing the same with the costumes. Dress the policemen in dark suits, but add open robes and/or Middle Eastern head coverings. **Coroner** could wear a white lab coat and Bible-time headgear; **Teenager** could combine casual clothes with a robe; **Woman** could mix Bible-time head covering with a contemporary outfit. If you can't find armor for the soldiers, give them robes and spears, and modern army helmets, if possible. Props include badges for **Joe** and **Bill** to flash and a small paper bag for **Bill**.

The Sound: If you're using stationary microphones, place one offstage, out of view of the audience, where **Joe** can deliver his voice-overs between appearances. You'll also need three onstage mikes near center stage. Plan your actors' movements so that they can deliver their onstage lines at these mikes. Provide the knocking sound effect by rapping on a piece of wood near your offstage mike. The brief scene-changing music should be reminiscent of the famous *Dragnet* theme *(Dum-da-DUM-dum...)*; this can be recorded or done live on a keyboard.

Other Options: Ancient Roman-type plastic armor (available from costume rental shops) will enhance the appearance of the **Soldiers**.

The Characters:

> **Joe Saturday**, deadpan police detective
> **Bill Sunday**, his talkative sidekick
> **Captain**, grimly self-important
> **Coroner**, breezy despite his job
> **Soldier One**, not too bright
> **Soldier Two**, no genius either
> **Teenager**, sincere and intense
> **Woman**, friendly and open

(As the skit begins, the stage is empty.)

Joe: *(Offstage, via sound system)* THIS...is the CITY. JERUSALEM, JUDEA. A lot of people LIVE here. A lot of people DIE here. But nobody LIVES here, DIES here, and then LIVES AGAIN here. NOBODY. I carry a BADGE. It's MY job to make sure the DE-CENT people in this town don't get misled by a lot of RELIGIOUS FANATICS. YOU know the type...spreading RUMORS...rumors about people RISING from the DEAD. My name's SATURDAY. My partner's BILL SUNDAY.

(Dragnet-type music.)

Joe: Monday, April 7, 10:20 a.m. We were at HEADQUARTERS, making out REPORTS on a small-time HOOD named BARABBAS.

(Joe and Bill enter and pantomime filling out papers. Captain enters.)

Captain: OK, boys! We've got ANOTHER one!

Joe: Oh, hi, Captain. Another WHAT?

Captain: RESURRECTION RUMOR. The CHIEF wants you to DROP whatever you're DOING and look INTO it. He wants you to get…

Joe: The FACTS?

Captain: RIGHT. Seems a RABBI was KILLED last FRIDAY.

Bill: MURDER, eh?

Captain: *(Shaking his head)* EXECUTION. CRIMINAL. Claimed to be a KING. Now the BODY'S missing. Rumor is he's ALIVE again.

Joe: That's a 512. THEFT and CONCEALMENT of a BODY with intent to perpetuate a RUMOR about a RESURRECTED RABBI.

Captain: *(Nodding)* The chief wants you to go the WHOLE NINE FURLONGS on this one, boys. RUMORS are flying, and he wants them STOPPED!

Joe: We'll do our BEST, Captain.

Captain: I know I can COUNT on you, boys. That's because you always get…

Joe: The FACTS?

Captain: RIGHT!

(Dragnet-type music. All exit.)

Joe: *(Offstage, via sound system)* Monday, April 7, 11:03 a.m. Our FIRST stop was the MORGUE.

(Coroner enters and busies himself in a corner. Joe and Bill enter opposite.)

Bill: Good IDEA, Joe. Looking for a BODY in the MORGUE, I mean. Reminds me of how I looked for a NEEDLE in a HAYSTACK when I was a KID. Got STRAW down my back. ITCHED like ANYTHING. Ever have that happen to YOU, Joe? You just ITCH and ITCH until you think you're going to go…

Joe: CRAZY?

Bill: Right.

Joe: Isn't that the CORONER?

Bill: Over in the CORNER?

Joe: What?

Bill: The CORONER…in the CORNER.

Joe: No TIME for that now. We've got to get…

Bill: The FACTS?

Joe: Right.

Coroner: HELLO, boys! You must be here about that POTTER'S FIELD case. *(He rolls out a large, imaginary drawer.)* Name was ISCARIOT. HANGED himself. What do you WANT with him?

Joe: We DON'T. We're after a RABBI…approximate age, 33. Died last FRIDAY.

Coroner: *(Shaking his head)* Nothing like that HERE, Joe. We had TWO THIEVES last Friday, but no RABBIS. SORRY. *(Coroner exits.)*

Bill: Guess the MORGUE is a DEAD END, Joe. Where to NOW?

Joe: The TOMB.

Bill: WHY, Joe?

(They look at each other.)

Joe: To get the FACTS.

(Dragnet-type music. They exit.)

Joe: *(Offstage, via sound system)* Monday, April 7, 4:13 p.m. We pulled up at a RICH MAN'S TOMB outside the CITY.

(Joe and Bill enter.)

Bill: These places give me the CREEPS, Joe…just like FUNERALS. My WIFE went to a funeral the other day. They had those little UNLEAVENED CRACKERS with OLIVES and MUSTARD SEEDS and things on them. She HATES green olives. You KNOW the kind, Joe? They're too…

Joe: Salty?

Bill: RIGHT. And…

Soldier One: HALT! This tomb is OFF-LIMITS, by order of the GOVERNOR!

(Joe and Bill flash their police badges.)

Soldier Two: COPS!

Soldier One: *(To Soldier Two)* Remember what we PRACTICED!

Soldier Two: Uh…WE don't know what happened! We were GUARDING the TOMB. It was all SEALED and EVERYTHING. Then we fell ASLEEP!

Soldier One: RIGHT! There was definitely NOT a man in a SHINING ROBE who appeared and SCARED us so much that we FAINTED.

Soldier Two: YEAH! The RABBI'S DISCIPLES came while we were ASLEEP and STOLE the BODY!

Soldier One: RIGHT! We know that because…because we were ASLEEP at the time!

Soldier Two: And nobody BRIBED us to say that or ANYTHING!

Bill: Makes sense to ME, Joe.

Joe: *(To Soldiers)* How do you know this rabbi was DEAD in the FIRST place?

Soldier Two: Oh, he was DEAD, all right! I checked him MYSELF, right after the EXECUTION.

Soldier One: So he COULDN'T have come back to life. We KNOW, because we were THERE!

Soldier Two: SLEEPING!

Bill: Well, Joe, there it IS! The rabbi's disciples STOLE the body! Guess that wraps it UP, eh?

Joe: Not QUITE. We're still missing ONE THING.

Bill: What's THAT, Joe?

Joe: The FACTS.

(Dragnet-type music. All exit.)

Joe: *(Offstage, via sound system)* Thursday, April 10, 2:14 p.m. We ran down a LEAD in EMMAUS. Two SUSPECTS had been seen proceeding down the ROAD…right after the RABBI'S BODY was stolen.

*(**Joe** and **Bill** enter.)*

Bill: You think they took the BODY, Joe?

Joe: Could BE. They're RELIGIOUS FANATICS. Watch your STEP.

*(They walk up to an imaginary door and pretend to knock. Sound of knocking. **Teenager** opens the "door." He smiles as **Joe** and **Bill** flash their badges.)*

Teenager: Come IN!

Joe: Son, were YOU on the ROAD to EMMAUS the other day?

Teenager: That's RIGHT! That's when we saw the…

Joe: Mind if we have a look AROUND?

Teenager: Go AHEAD. ANYWAY, we saw the…

Bill: *(Opening imaginary closet door and peering inside)* There's no rabbi in HERE, Joe.

Teenager: We SAW the rabbi! The one who died last FRIDAY! I was on the road with a FRIEND, and we SAW him. He's ALIVE!

*(**Joe** and **Bill** look at each other, then shake their heads.)*

Joe: Consumption of NEW WINE by a MINOR. That's against the LAW, son.

Teenager: But I didn't…

Bill: It's a 427, Joe…I think.

Joe: It's always the same STORY with you kids. You go out and get yourself full of NEW WINE and end up seeing DEAD RABBIS walking down the ROAD. It's a SHAME, a real SHAME.

Teenager: But we SAW him! We didn't RECOGNIZE him at first. Then right before he DISAPPEARED…

Joe: DISAPPEARED?

Teenager: That's RIGHT. He VANISHED into THIN AIR!

(As before, Joe and Bill look at each other, then shake their heads.)

Teenager: You—you don't BELIEVE me!

Joe: There's only ONE thing WE believe, son.

Bill: The FACTS, Joe?

Joe: The FACTS.

(Dragnet-type music. All exit.)

Joe: *(Offstage, via sound system)* Tuesday, April 15, 9:48 p.m. We STAKED OUT the UPPER ROOM. Word was that the rabbi's DISCIPLES had been HIDING there…probably hiding the stolen BODY there, too. We PARKED in a nearby ALLEY and WATCHED as a sleazy collection of FISHERMEN, WOMEN, ZEALOTS, and TAX COLLECTORS went into the place, ONE by ONE.

(Joe and Bill enter and stand as if watching a nearby building.)

Bill: As long as we're WAITING, Joe, you mind if I have a BITE? *(He takes a small paper bag out of his pocket.)* My WIFE made it, Joe. BARLEY CAKES and FIGS. Don't CARE for FIGS. Too WRINKLY. I like those OTHER things, those…

Joe: DATES?

Bill: RIGHT.

Joe: Okay. Let's MOVE IN.

Bill: Can I finish my BARLEY CAKES, Joe? I'll…

(They look at each other.)

Bill: RIGHT, Joe. After we get…

Joe: The FACTS.

(Dragnet-type music. They exit.)

Joe: *(Offstage, via sound system)* Tuesday, April 15, 9:59 p.m. It sounded like a PARTY was going on in the UPPER ROOM.

*(**Joe** and **Bill** enter. They walk up to an imaginary door and pretend to knock. Sound of knocking. **Woman** enters and opens the door.)*

Woman: YES?

Joe: *(Flashing his badge)* POLICE officers. We have a few QUESTIONS.

Woman: CERTAINLY! What would you like to KNOW?

Joe: *(His eyes narrowing)* Just the FACTS, ma'am.

Woman: Well, come right IN! *(She motions them in and exits opposite. **Joe** and **Bill** enter the room.)*

Joe: *(Holding up his badge and addressing imaginary crowd)* Party's OVER, folks! You're all under ARREST for THEFT and CONCEALMENT of a BODY with INTENT to PER- PETUATE a RUMOR about a RESURRECTED RABBI. You have the RIGHT to remain SILENT. You have the RIGHT to…

Bill: SAY, Joe…how come nobody's LISTENING?

Joe: Looks like they're too busy CELEBRATING something.

Bill: Who's that guy they're all TALKING to? They keep calling him RABBI.

Joe: About 33 years old, wearing a WHITE ROBE. NASTY SCAR in the PALM of each HAND, just like he'd been…

*(**Joe** and **Bill** look at each other.)*

Bill: It's HIM, Joe!

Joe: That's RIGHT.

Bill: He doesn't look DEAD to ME, Joe.

Joe: No, he DOESN'T.

Bill: What do we do NOW, Joe?

Joe: (*Sighing*) You know PROCEDURE. We make our REPORT.

Bill: But, JOE…

Joe: I KNOW. There's just one PROBLEM.

Bill: What's THAT, Joe?

Joe: The FACTS. Just the FACTS.

(*Dragnet-type music. They exit.*)

Joe: (*Offstage, via sound system*) Wednesday, April 16, 10:17 a.m. We finished making our REPORT to the CAPTAIN.

(**Joe**, **Bill**, and **Captain** enter.)

Captain: SO, boys…the RABBI'S FOLLOWERS STOLE the BODY, eh?

Joe: Yes, SIR. SMUGGLED it out of the COUNTRY. WAY out. Out of our JURISDICTION.

Bill: They DID? But, JOE, I thought…(**Joe** elbows him in the ribs.) OW!

Captain: It's just as WELL. The whole thing will BLOW OVER in a WEEK or two ANYWAY.

Joe: (*Nodding*) No doubt ABOUT it, sir.

Captain: But how about all those SIGHTINGS? What made SO MANY PEOPLE claim to have seen this man ALIVE?

Bill: YEAH, Joe, how…

Joe: Mass HYPNOSIS, sir…SWAMP gas…HYSTERIA. It's ALL in the REPORT.

Bill: Oh. I guess we were…

Joe: MISTAKEN?

Bill: Uh, RIGHT.

Captain: Good WORK, BOYS. I KNEW I could count on you to get...

Joe: The FACTS?

Captain: NO! A REASONABLE-SOUNDING EXPLANATION!

Bill: Makes sense to ME, Joe.

Joe: *(Sighing)* It WOULD.

(Dragnet-type music. All exit.)

Related Scriptures:
- Luke 24
- 1 Corinthians 15:1-20
- Philippians 3:10-11

Related Topics:
- Easter
- Faith and reason
- Reliability of the Bible

Trial of the Century

Topic: Guilt

The Scene: A courtroom

The Simple Setup: For the **Judge**, place one table center stage with a chair behind it facing the audience; for the **Defendant**, put a table downstage right with a chair in front of it, facing toward center stage. For **Prosecutor**, put a table downstage left with a chair in front of it, facing toward center stage. Make sure **Defendant** and **Prosecutor** aren't put in a position to turn their backs to the audience, especially while speaking. **Judge** should wear a judicial-looking black robe, such as a choir robe or graduation gown; **Defendant** can wear casual clothes; **Prosecutor** should wear a suit; **Bailiff** should wear khaki or blue shirt and slacks, with a badge on the shirt. Props include a pair of gloves that fit **Defendant** and a gavel for **Judge**.

The Sound: If you're using stationary microphones, set one at each of the three tables.

Other Options: If possible, make the **Judge**'s table look more imposing by "paneling" the sides with cardboard.

The Characters:
>   **Judge**, guilt-ridden and weepy
>   **Prosecutor**, much like the **Judge**
>   **Defendant**, a pugnacious thug
>   **Bailiff**, straightforward and stoic

*(As the skit begins, **Defendant** sits at table stage right, **Prosecutor** sits at table stage left, and **Bailiff** stands next to table center stage.)*

Bailiff: *(Loudly, looking straight ahead)* The case of the PEOPLE VERSUS T.J. SIMKINS…the honorable JUDGE MORRIS BURRITO presiding. ALL RISE.

*(**Defendant** and **Prosecutor** stand.)*

Judge: *(Rushing in, on the verge of tears)* Oh, I'm so SORRY I'm LATE! *(Sits at center table.)* Please, PLEASE, sit DOWN. *(**Defendant** and **Prosecutor** sit.)* I was SURE I set my ALARM last night. I must have pushed the wrong BUTTON. OH, this is INEXCUSABLE! THREE MINUTES LATE! I'm so SORRY. *(Blows nose loudly, then composes self somewhat.)* Now, WHERE did we LEAVE OFF yesterday?

Prosecutor: *(Standing up, on the verge of tears)* Your HONOR, we were about to see whether the GLOVES worn in this QUADRUPLE AX MURDER fit on the defendant's HANDS.

*(**Defendant** stands, rolls eyes, and puts hands in the air, chest-high, as if waiting for gloves.)*

Judge: OH, yes. I'M sorry. I should have REMEMBERED. I should have WRITTEN IT DOWN. I'm so FORGETFUL! It's a TERRIBLE FAULT. I hope you can find it in your heart to FORGIVE me!

Prosecutor: *(Sniffling)* Oh, your honor…that's NOTHING compared to the HORRIBLE thing I did this MORNING! I was in a HURRY, and when I BACKED the CAR out of the DRIVEWAY, I—I RAN OVER the MORNING PAPER!

Judge: OH, my WORD!

Prosecutor: There were TIRE TRACKS all over the FRONT PAGE! It was practically UNREADABLE! I've PRAYED for FORGIVENESS, but the BURDEN of GUILT is so OVERWHELMING.

Defendant: HEY! I'm gettin' tired of STANDING HERE with my HANDS in the air! Are we gonna get this SHOW on the ROAD, or WHAT?

Prosecutor: Oh, I'M sorry…SO sorry! Here I am going on about my sickening SHORTCOMINGS, WASTING your valuable TIME! What was I THINKING?

Defendant: Beats ME! This is very INCONVENIENT…almost as bad as when I had to give you a little piece of my HAIR for that stupid DNA TEST!

Prosecutor: Oh, YES, I KNOW! That must have been AWFUL for you! And you probably felt EMBARRASSED when your DNA matched the sample found at the SCENE OF THE CRIME!

Judge: *(Sniffling)* I'm SURE it was all a MISTAKE!

Defendant: You got THAT right! You never should have brought it up in the FIRST place! Or that LIE DETECTOR TEST I flunked! That was supposed to be a SECRET!

Judge: Oh, why couldn't I keep QUIET about that? I'm such a BLABBERMOUTH! *(Hitting self on the head repeatedly with the gavel between each word)* I…CAN'T…SEEM…TO…CHANGE!

Defendant: And all those WITNESSES who saw me SHARPENING THE AX right before the MURDERS! How do you think that made ME feel?

Prosecutor: Oh, I've been so INSENSITIVE! I know I can NEVER make it UP to you.

Judge: All I can do is have that silly TESTIMONY stricken from the RECORD. *(Addressing unseen note-taker)* The COURT REPORTER will STRIKE from the record ALL NEGATIVE REFERENCES to the Defendant. Oh, I know that's EXTRA WORK for the court reporter…so sorry to DO that to you…I have no RIGHT…

Defendant: YEAH, yeah. So where are the GLOVES, already?

Prosecutor: Right HERE. Please pardon the DELAY. I've ALWAYS had a problem with PUNCTUALITY. I'm SURE it's the UNFORGIVEABLE SIN.

(Prosecutor puts gloves on Defendant's hands; they fit.)

Defendant: HEY, a PERFECT FIT! I was WONDERIN' what happened to these gloves. I can KEEP 'em now, right?

Prosecutor: Of COURSE! It's the LEAST we can do!

Judge: If the GLOVES FIT, I must ACQUIT…or SOMETHING like that. The DEFENDANT is FREE TO GO! *(Pounds gavel on table.)*

Defendant: WELL, it's about TIME! *(Exits smugly.)*

Judge: But I sentence MYSELF to LIFE IN PRISON with NO POSSIBILITY FOR PAROLE! I'm GUILTY! GUILTY, I tell you!

Prosecutor: Oh, so am I, your honor! For my HEINOUS CRIMES, the PROSECUTION requests the DEATH PENALTY!

Judge: OK! *(Pounds gavel on table.)* Bailiff, take us AWAY!

(Judge and Prosecutor each offer an arm to Bailiff, who starts to lead them away.)

Prosecutor: *(To Bailiff)* I'm so SORRY to be a BOTHER like this! I hope my ARM isn't too HEAVY!

Judge: *(To Bailiff)* I'm sure you have BETTER things to do! Please FORGIVE me!

(Shaking head, Bailiff leads Judge and Prosecutor away as they wail uncontrollably.)

► **Related Scriptures:**
  ● Psalm 103:8-18
  ● Romans 8:1-4
  ● 1 John 1:9-2:2

► **Related Topics:**
  ● Sin
  ● Grace
  ● Forgiveness

The Whole Armor

Topic: Spiritual Warfare

The Scene: A clothing shop

The Simple Setup: For the store counter, set up a table with a large tablecloth or sheet over it. Place several cardboard boxes on the table. One box should contain a wide leather belt, a narrower belt, and a piece of string; another box should contain a red shirt, a pair of dark sunglasses, and a can of hair spray or air freshener. (Cover the label.) The other boxes can be empty. Additional props include a toy bow and arrow and a large shopping bag for **Salesperson**; a piece of paper (the list), a checkbook, and a pen for **Customer**. Costume for **Salesperson** should be a suit, perhaps with a flower in the lapel; **Customer**'s clothes can be casual.

The Sound: If you're using stationary microphones, place one on each side of the table. To produce the sound of the clattering metal armor, drop a few pots and pans into a large box near an offstage mike. Salesperson can deliver his or her offstage line about the Breastplate of Righteousness at the same mike.

Other Options: To make the set more realistic, place a rack of clothes on the stage, and fasten a couple of "SALE" signs to the wall.

The Characters:
    Customer, naive and eager
    Salesperson, a silver-tongued deceiver

(Salesperson stands at a table on which several boxes are arranged. Enter Customer, carrying a piece of paper.)

Salesperson: May I HELP you?

Customer: *(Glancing around)* I'm LOOKING for an OUTFIT. I was headed for ANOTHER shop, but it's too far AWAY, and I was getting TIRED...

Salesperson: PERFECTLY understandable. I'm SURE we can help you with ANY items you could have found at that OTHER store. *(Rubs hands together.)* And at a better PRICE, no doubt.

Customer: I HOPE so! I hear the prices at that OTHER store are pretty HIGH. They want practically EVERYTHING you've GOT!

Salesperson: Tsk, tsk. Imagine the NERVE of that other store, claiming to be the only OFFICIAL outfitter... and then charging an ARM and a LEG! Now, what SORT of outfit would you LIKE?

Customer: A SUIT of ARMOR.

Salesperson: A suit of WHAT?

Customer: ARMOR! See, I just JOINED UP to FIGHT THE BATTLE, and they gave me this LIST of ARMOR I'm supposed to wear. *(Holds up the piece of paper.)*

Salesperson: *(Squinting at list)* Oh, THAT armor! Of COURSE. We have an old suit like that in the BACK, I believe. But take my WORD for it…you wouldn't LIKE it.

Customer: Why NOT?

Salesperson: *(With a sniff)* It's simply GAUCHE! No one would be caught DEAD in a suit like that THESE days!

Customer: But I'm supposed to GET one. "Put on the WHOLE ARMOR," they told me. They said I couldn't fight the battle WITHOUT it!

Salesperson: *(Sighing)* Oh, very WELL. What do you need FIRST?

Customer: *(Consulting list)* The GIRDLE OF TRUTH.

Salesperson: A GIRDLE?

Customer: Well…I…It says right HERE that I have to GIRD MY LOINS with TRUTH. Have you GOT one or NOT?

Salesperson: Just a MINUTE! *(Pulls a wide leather belt from a box and hands it to Customer.)* HERE.

Customer: *(Cinching it around waist)* OUCH! It feels awfully TIGHT. Haven't you got it in a LARGER SIZE?

Salesperson: SORRY. You know how TRUTH is…one size supposedly fits ALL! So CONSTRICTING, don't you think?

Customer: Yeah, I guess. But they said I had to GIRD UP MY LOINS, so…

Salesperson: We DO have an ALTERNATIVE. It's the BELT OF REGULATIONS. *(Pulls a narrower belt from the box and hands it over.)* A LOVELY piece of work, STUDDED with ARTIFICIAL DO'S AND DON'TS!

Customer: *(Trying it on)* OW! THIS one's even WORSE! It's so TIGHT I can barely BREATHE!

Salesperson: Some PREFER that HIDEBOUND feeling. But I have something ELSE that may be more to your LIKING. *(Pulls a piece of string from the box and holds it up.)*

Customer: What's THAT?

Salesperson: The SASH OF SINCERITY! Try it ON. I think you'll find it quite COMFORTABLE.

Customer: *(Putting it around waist)* Feels FINE! *(Frowns.)* But they told me I couldn't FIGHT THE BATTLE if I didn't GIRD UP MY...

Salesperson: EXACTLY! How can you fight a BATTLE with a TIGHT OLD BELT around your waist? You need room to MOVE, to SLIDE, to WAFFLE! The SASH OF SINCERITY is every BIT as good as the GIRDLE OF TRUTH...and a lot more FASHIONABLE. Who needs TRUTH if you're SINCERE?

Customer: Well...I guess that makes SENSE. I'll TAKE the sash.

Salesperson: An EXCELLENT choice! What's NEXT?

Customer: *(Checking list)* The BREASTPLATE OF RIGHTEOUSNESS.

Salesperson: UGH!

Customer: What's the MATTER?

Salesperson: You'll absolutely HATE it...an UGLY old thing, probably RUSTY by now...weighs a TON...been out of style for AGES.

Customer: But my LIST says...

Salesperson: *(Sighing)* I KNOW, I KNOW. *(Exits. Sound of metal clattering. **Salesperson**, huffing and puffing, calls from offstage.)* SEE? I can't even drag the monstrosity onto the SALES FLOOR!

Customer: It DOES look kind of UNCOMFORTABLE. *(**Salesperson** returns, dusting self off.)* But how could I go into battle WITHOUT it?

Salesperson: *(Snapping fingers)* By wearing the STRAITJACKET of SELF-righteousness! *(Opens a box and holds it in front of **Customer**.)* What do you THINK?

Customer: It looks LIGHTER than that IRON thing. But I don't think I could FIGHT too well without my HANDS. *(Reaches into the box.)* Feels kind of STIFF, too...like a STUFFED SHIRT!

Salesperson: I know EXACTLY what you mean! *(Reaches into another box and pulls out a red shirt.)* Try THIS instead.

Customer: Hey, I LIKE this! But how can it replace the BREASTPLATE OF RIGHTEOUSNESS?

Salesperson: *(Chuckling)* Look at the INSIGNIA over the POCKET.

Customer: *(Squinting)* Is it an ALLIGATOR?

Salesperson: NO! It's a SMILEY FACE! The INTERNATIONAL SYMBOL of...

Customer: RIGHTEOUSNESS?

Salesperson: No, NICENESS! It's the SPORTS SHIRT OF NICENESS. A PERFECT SUBSTITUTE. And with that BRIGHT RED COLOR, the ENEMY will NEVER notice you sneaking through the FOREST!

Customer: Really?

Salesperson: *(Rubbing hands together)* TRUST me!

Customer: *(Checking list)* The SHOES OF THE GOSPEL...

Salesperson: *(Holding another open box in front of **Customer**)* Right HERE...the most UNATTRAC-TIVE footwear known to MAN! Wouldn't you rather wear those NICE shoes you've got ON?

Customer: Yes, I guess I WOULD. But they TOLD me...

Salesperson: Of COURSE they did! They were probably JEALOUS of your FINE SHOES! Let me show you what you REALLY need...the SHOESTRINGS of the Gospel. *(Holds another open box in front of **Customer**.)* Laces with tiny CROSSES printed all over them! You can wear your OWN shoes and make a STATEMENT at the same TIME! Aren't they MARVELOUS?

Customer: Well, OK. *(Consulting list)* Now I need the SHIELD OF FAITH.

Salesperson: You may need FAITH...but you DON'T need a SHIELD! NOBODY'S used a shield for CENTURIES! War isn't fought with BOWS AND ARROWS anymore. This is the ATOMIC AGE!

Customer: Oh! Then what do I NEED?

Salesperson: The SUNGLASSES of Faith! For SHIELDING YOUR EYES on the BATTLEFIELD! Here, try THESE. *(Gives **Customer** a pair of sunglasses.)*

Customer: *(Trying them on)* I can't see a THING! These sunglasses are PITCH BLACK!

Salesperson: NATURALLY! They're for BLIND faith!

Customer: I can't go into BATTLE with THESE! Guess I'll have to stick with the SHIELD.

Salesperson: You want a SHIELD? I'll GIVE you a shield. But not one of those big BRONZE things! Have a BUTTON instead! *(Holds another open box in front of **Customer**.)* They're SHAPED like shields, only much SMALLER. You can pin them right on your SHIRT. They're the BUTTONS OF BELIEF!

Customer: But I need FAITH!

Salesperson: FAITH, BELIEF…they're all the SAME! Just look at the wonderful SLOGANS on these buttons.

Customer: *(Pointing into the box)* I like THIS one. It says, "MAKE BELIEVE, NOT WAR."

Salesperson: It's YOU!

Customer: *(Reading from list)* Next, the HELMET OF SALVATION.

Salesperson: Take my WORD for it…wearing that HELMET is like having a GALVANIZED BUCKET on your head! Anyway, what's REALLY the IMPORTANT thing about SALVATION?

Customer: Spending ETERNITY with…

Salesperson: NO! SECURITY is what everybody wants! And that's exactly what you GET with the HEADBAND OF SECURITY! *(Holds an open box in front of **Customer**.)* Absorbent TERRY CLOTH! Keeps you DRY in the heat of BATTLE! THAT'S the kind of protection you REALLY need!

Customer: A HEADBAND? I don't KNOW…seems like…

Salesperson: *(Pulling a spray can from box)* Then try the HAIR SPRAY OF HOLINESS. SO much lighter than that miserable HELMET!

Customer: HOLINESS, huh? They TOLD me I'd need THAT, too.

Salesperson: It's ARTIFICIAL, of course. But who'll know the DIFFERENCE? *(Sprays the hair spray in* *the air near Customer.)* LOOK at that! Makes a lovely HALO EFFECT when the LIGHT hits it just right, don't you THINK?

Customer: Yes, but…I'll take the HEADBAND.

Salesperson: Very GOOD. That leaves—don't tell me—the SWORD OF THE SPIRIT!

Customer: Right.

Salesperson: MUCH too EXPENSIVE, I'm afraid. Fine for MUSEUMS, but not much ELSE. I have something BETTER!

Customer: What's THAT?

Salesperson: *(Holding an open box before Customer)* The BRASS KNUCKLES OF DOCTRINE! They don't PIERCE quite like the old SWORDS did, but they're WONDERFUL for PUMMELLING!

Customer: I could really use something SHARPER. After all, this is WAR!

Salesperson: SHARPER? Of COURSE! What you need is the TIE TACK OF TOLERANCE! *(Holding open box before Customer)* Our designers have managed to REDUCE the Sword of the Spirit to THIS size for ORNAMENTAL purposes. But of course there's still a bit of a STICKPIN on the back!

Customer: I could never do battle with THIS! It would barely draw BLOOD!

Salesperson: *(Shuddering)* BLOOD? We are talking about FASHION here! Just THINK of it. You'll be the envy of EVERYONE on the BATTLEFIELD. You've got the SASH OF SINCERITY, the SPORTS SHIRT OF NICENESS, the SHOESTRINGS OF THE GOSPEL, the BUTTON OF BELIEF, the HEADBAND OF SECURITY, and the TIE TACK OF TOLERANCE! What MORE could any soldier WANT?

Customer: *(Looking into the boxes)* I WILL look pretty good, WON'T I? OK. I'll take the WHOLE ARMOR…er, OUTFIT.

Salesperson: EXCELLENT! Will that be CASH or CHARGE?

Customer: CHECK. *(Pulls out a checkbook and pen.)* Who do I make it OUT to?

Salesperson: *(Rubbing hands together)* B.L. ZEEBUB.

(Salesperson puts the boxes in a large bag. Customer finishes the check, hands it over, and picks up the bag.)

Customer: I'll put these on as SOON as I get HOME!

Salesperson: Oh, GOOD! That will make things SO much EASIER!

Customer: Well, THANKS! *(Turns to go.)* Glad I came HERE instead of that OTHER store! *(Exits.)*

Salesperson: *(Taking a small bow and arrow from behind the counter and aiming it in the direction of* **Customer***)* So am I! *(Still aiming bow and arrow, starts toward the same exit* **Customer** *took.)* So…am…I! *(***Salesperson** *exits.)*

▶ **Related Scriptures:**
- Ephesians 6:10-17
- James 4:7
- 1 Peter 5:8-9

▶ **Related Topics:**
- Temptation
- Resisting the devil
- Discipleship

The Workout Service

Topic: Worship

The Scene: A health club

The Simple Setup: No set is needed. The **Leader** will need a boom box and three tapes: one cued to a rock song; one cued to a piece of slower, traditional music like country or swing; and one cued to lively classical music. All songs should be secular rather than spiritual. If you want to play the music through your sound system rather than the boom box, have **Leader** go through the motions of playing the tapes. **Usher** may read the "call to work out" from a real or imaginary book.

The Sound: If you're using stationary microphones, put one center stage for the **Leader**, flanked on both sides by a mike for **Older Persons** and one for **Younger Persons**. The **Usher** can go to one of the side mikes to deliver his or her lines. If you want to play the music through the sound system, it's easiest to put the song excerpts on a single tape, as long as you time them correctly.

Other Options: Add depth to the skit by having the actors wear sweat suits or other workout gear.

The Characters:

    Leader, an energetic and friendly aerobics instructor
    Usher, the instructor's assistant
    Older Person One, cranky and slow-moving
    Older Person Two, also cranky and slow-moving
    Younger Person One, fidgety and impatient
    Younger Person Two, also fidgety and impatient

*(**Usher** stands at one side of the stage, near the real or imaginary door through which the others will enter. As **Older** and **Younger Persons** enter, **Usher** greets them.)*

Usher: WELCOME to the HEALTH CLUB! So nice to SEE you! Glad you could be WITH us today! The WORKOUT SERVICE will begin in just a MOMENT.

*(**Usher** stays near the entrance as the others take their places—the **Older** players stage left and the **Younger** stage right. **All** face audience. Finally the **Leader** enters, carrying a boom box and tapes, and stands center stage, facing audience.)*

Leader: WELCOME to the WORKOUT SERVICE! Please TAKE a moment to extend a HAND OF GREETING to those who have JOINED you for today's WORKOUT!

*(**Older Person One** and **Older Person Two** shake hands only with each other; **Younger Person One** and **Younger Person Two** shake hands only with each other. **Younger** and **Older** give each other disgusted looks.)*

Leader: THANK you. And now, hear our CALL TO WORK OUT.

Usher: *(Reading from a book)* I was GLAD when they said unto me, "Let us go into the GYM and WORK OUT." *(Usher exits.)*

Leader: THANK you! Let's begin with a WARM-UP! *(Leader starts playing the rock song on the boom box.)* Ready? Let's do some STRETCHES! *(Leader starts stretching.)* And a ONE, two, three, four! ONE, two, three, four!

*(The **Younger** join in the stretching. The **Older** just stand there.)*

Older One: WHOA! STOP!

*(Everyone stops. The **Leader** stops the tape.)*

Older Two: I can't STAND that music! It's too LOUD! GUITARS don't put me in the MOOD for a WORKOUT!

Older One: That's RIGHT! NO GUITARS!

Younger One: Oh, BROTHER!

Older Two: WHAT was that? WHAT did you say?

Younger One: I said, "AMEN, BROTHER!"

Older Two: Oh.

Leader: Uh…let's try something ELSE. *(Puts in tape of slower, old-fashioned music and starts it.)* Ready? Let's WARM UP! *(Leader starts stretching.)* And a STRETCH, two, three, four! STRETCH, two, three, four!

*(The **Older** join in the stretching. The **Younger** just stand there.)*

Younger One: HEY! Knock it OFF!

*(Everyone stops. The **Leader** stops the tape.)*

Younger Two: What kind of warm-up music is THAT? It's too OLD-FASHIONED! It needs to be FASTER!

Younger One: RIGHT! FASTER!

Older One: What about my ARTHRITIS? Disrespectful young WHIPPERSNAPPERS!

Younger Two: HUH? WHAT did you say?

Older One: I said, "The ZIPPER'S caught on my WINDBREAKER!"

Younger Two: Oh.

Leader: Well—let's try a DIFFERENT tape. *(Puts in a tape of fast-paced classical music and starts it.)* Ready? WARM UP! *(**Leader** starts stretching.)* And STRETCH, two, three, four! STRETCH, two, three, four!

*(The **Older** join in the stretching. The **Younger** just stand there.)*

Younger Two: WHOA! HOLD IT!

*(Everyone stops. The **Leader**, getting irritated, stops the tape.)*

Leader: NOW what?

Younger One: THAT'S no good! It's even older than the LAST music!

Younger Two: YEAH! This isn't the DORK Ages!

Older One: DARK Ages, you brainless BRAT!

Younger One: WHAT did you say?

Older One: I FORGOT to feed the CAT!

Younger One: Oh.

Leader: Well, let's try THIS again. *(Puts in the rock tape again and starts it.)* Ready? Warm up! *(**Leader** starts stretching.)* And a STRETCH, two, three, four! STRETCH, two, three, four!

*(The **Younger** join in the stretching. The **Older** just stand there.)*

Older One: AAUGGH! My EARS!

*(Everyone stops. The **Leader**, exasperated, stops the tape.)*

Older Two: You already PLAYED that! We HATE that music!

Older One: Get RID of that awful NOISE!

Younger One: HEY! Some of us LIKE that music! You can't make us listen to your OLD stuff!

Older Two: We want OUR kind of music!

Younger Two: Then go to a MUSEUM!

Older One: WHAT did you say?

Younger Two: I said, "YOU BELONG IN A MUSEUM!"

Older Two: Oh. *(Pauses.)* Now, just a MINUTE, you…

Leader: STOP! QUIET!!!

*(**All** quiet down.)*

Leader: Why are you ARGUING? You didn't come here for a CONCERT! You came to WORK OUT!

Older One: WHAT?

Older Two: What are you TALKING about?

Younger One: WE didn't come here to WORK OUT!

Younger Two: We came here to watch YOU work out!

Older One: Working out is YOUR job, not OURS!

Younger One: All WE have to do is a little WARM-UP!

Older One: *(To **Leader**)* So now that YOU'RE warmed up, start EXERCISING!

Younger Two: JUMPING JACKS! ONE, two, three, four!

Older Two: And take TEN LAPS around the BUILDING while you're at it!

Youngers and Olders: YEAH!

*(**Leader** shakes head and jogs out of the room.)*

Younger One: WELL! We finally found something we could AGREE on!

Older One: *(To Younger One)* Gimme FIVE, dude! *(He/she does so.)*

Younger Two: I LOVE workouts, don't YOU?

Older Two: Makes me feel FIT as a FIDDLE!

Younger One: Let's do this EVERY week!

All: YEAH!

(All exit.)

▶ **Related Scriptures:**
- Psalm 95
- John 4:19-24
- Romans 14

▶ **Related Topics:**
- Church unity
- Clashes over personal convictions
- Being a disciple instead of a spectator

The Cubicle

Topic: Patience

The Scene: An office

The Simple Setup: For this spoof of the comic strip *Dilbert*, you'll need a desk and chair. If possible, add a computer to the desk. For props, **Filbert** will need a piece of paper and a Bible, and **Malice** will need a large manila envelope containing several pieces of paper. For costumes, try to imitate the appearance of the corresponding *Dilbert* characters. Ideally, **Filbert** should have a crew cut, heavy-rimmed glasses, white shirt, necktie that curls up at the bottom, and dark slacks. **Boss** should wear a dark suit and have large, dark tufts of hair that stick out and up from the sides of his otherwise bald head. (Use a clown-type bald cap from a costume shop if you're ambitious.) **Wiley** should wear a white shirt, tie, and slacks; **Malice** should wear a suit and have a severe "helmet" hairstyle. If you can't match the *Dilbert* characters, though, don't worry. Note that the actor who plays **Filbert** should silently emote and gesture as the voice of his thoughts reads his lines at an offstage microphone.

The Sound: If you're using stationary microphones, put one offstage. Place another near the desk (for **Filbert**'s visitors) and one near the exit.

Other Options: If you can get three cubicle walls to surround the desk (except in the front), it would make the scene even more Dilbertian.

The Characters:

    Filbert, mild-mannered office worker

    Voice of Filbert's Thoughts

    The Boss, dense and demanding male

    Wiley, lazy and deceitful male employee

    Malice, sarcastic and resentful female employee

*(As the skit begins, **Filbert** is reading a piece of paper at his desk. We hear his thoughts via the sound system.)*

Voice of Filbert's Thoughts: "MEMO. From: MANAGEMENT. To: FILBERT. Due to recent CUTBACKS, all future MEMOS will be known only as "MEMS." This will SAVE an average of 300 O's per MONTH, which look much like ZEROES and can be ATTACHED to OTHER numbers, thereby turning profits of 5 PERCENT into profits of 5 MILLION percent. THANK you." *(Pauses.)* Why do they DO these things? How can I stand to WORK here? *(Pauses.)* PATIENCE, Filbert. Remember what the PASTOR said at CHURCH: "A PATIENT man has great UNDERSTANDING, but a QUICK-TEMPERED man displays FOLLY." Proverbs 14:29. Got to REMEMBER that…got to REMEMBER.

*(Enter **Wiley**, walking gingerly as if his feet hurt.)*

Wiley: HI, Filbert!

**Voice of Filbert's
Thoughts:** Oh, NO...it's WILEY.

Wiley: SO, Filbert! I just figured out a NEW WAY to STEAL OFFICE SUPPLIES. You fill your SOCKS with STAPLES! OUCH! Works with PUSHPINS, too! Well, see you LATER! *(Exiting gingerly)* OW! OUCH! OWEE!

**Voice of Filbert's
Thoughts:** Sure beats WORKING, DOESN'T it, Wiley? What a hunk of DEADWOOD! Why do I have to carry HIS weight and MINE, TOO? It's not FAIR! (Pauses.) Oops. Have to be PATIENT. *(**Filbert** takes Bible from desk and flips through it.)* I need another VERSE. *(**Filbert** stops at a page.)* "A man's WISDOM gives him PATIENCE; it is to his GLORY to overlook an OFFENSE." Proverbs 19:11. THERE. I feel BETTER.

*(Enter **Malice**. She carries a large manila envelope.)*

Malice: FILBERT!

**Voice of Filbert's
Thoughts:** Oh, HI, MALICE. I was HOPING you'd come by with another of your ENLIGHTENING TIRADES.

Malice: You engineers are a SUBHUMAN form of LIFE! You are DEVOID of SENSITIVITY! *(She holds up envelope.)* I passed around an ENVELOPE trying to get you guys to buy my niece's CHIPMUNK SCOUT CANDIES, and WHAT HAPPENS? *(She pulls papers from envelope.)* You put in copies of INTERNET POSTINGS about how CANDY ROTS YOUR TEETH! Well, maybe YOU didn't...but the OTHER engineers did, and they're all AWAY FROM THEIR DESKS playing VIDEO GAMES in the ARCADE across the STREET! *(She throws papers at him.)* Take THAT, you...you...ENGINEER! *(She exits.)*

**Voice of Filbert's
Thoughts:** PATIENCE. *(**Filbert** flips desperately through Bible)* PATIENCE...need...BIBLE VERSE. *(**Filbert** stops at a page.)* Uh..."Clothe yourselves with COMPASSION, KINDNESS, HUMIL-ITY, GENTLENESS and PATIENCE." Colossians 3:12. RUNNING...OUT OF...VERSES.

*(Enter **Boss**.)*

Boss: FILBERT! Uh...that IS your NAME, isn't it?

**Voice of Filbert's
Thoughts:** Oh, GREAT! The BOSS! Just what I NEED right now!

Boss: FILBERT, I'm instituting a new EMPLOYEE EXCELLENCE INCENTIVE PLAN!

Voice of Filbert's Thoughts: UH-oh.

Boss: From THIS day FORWARD, ANY EMPLOYEE judged by ME to have displayed EX-CELLENCE will be REWARDED by having the letter "E" PAINFULLY BRANDED ON HIS OR HER FOREHEAD with a RED-HOT IRON! And to kick it all OFF, I want YOU to be the FIRST one BRANDED as an EXAMPLE to the REST! Be in the FURNACE ROOM at 3:15! *(To himself, as he leaves)* I LOVE to see those BURNING COALS of GRATITUDE in their eyes! *(**Boss** exits.)*

Voice of Filbert's Thoughts: *(As **Filbert** flips frantically through Bible)* BIBLE verse! QUICK! Must have verse about PA-TIENCE! *(**Filbert** stops at a page.)* "If ONLY you would SLAY the WICKED...AWAY from me, you BLOODTHIRSTY MEN!" Psalm 139:19. No, no, not THAT one! *(**Filbert** flips frantically through Bible, then stops at a page.)* Uh..."May they be THROWN into the FIRE, into MIRY PITS, NEVER to RISE." Psalm 140:10. NO! *(Enter **Wiley**, **Malice**, and **Boss**, who pantomime talking to each other near the exit.)* HEAD SPINNING...got to get OUT before I...become...crazed...madman! AAUGGHH! *(As **Voice** screams, **Filbert** gets up and runs out through the exit, bumping into the others on the way and nearly knocking them over.)*

Boss: WELL!

Wiley: WOW! HE was in a hurry!

Malice: How RUDE! If you ask ME, he needs to learn a little...PATIENCE!

*(**Boss** and **Malice** nod in agreement as all three exit in a huff.)*

▶ **Related Scriptures:**
- Proverbs 19:1
- Matthew 18:21-35
- James 1:19; 5:7-11

▶ **Related Topics:**
- Faith in the workplace
- Stress
- Living in harmony

King of the World

Topic: Pride

The Scene: A ship at sea

The Simple Setup: This is a takeoff on the movie *Titanic*. Place three chairs stage right in a tight semi-circle, facing the audience. Place two more chairs stage left, facing left. Props include two identical, inexpensive necklaces (preferably with pendants); a sketch pad and a pencil; two sheets of paper from the sketch pad; and a purse. Costumes for **Young Rosie** and **Zack** should look old-fashioned; clothes for **Treasure Hunter** and **Assistant** should be contemporary casual. **Elderly Rosie** should wear a long traditional dress. To help **Elderly Rosie** look her age, you may want to add wrinkles with eyeliner, powder her hair with cornstarch, and put it up in a bun. She could walk with a cane, too.

The Sound: If you're using stationary microphones, put one in front of each chair. If at all possible, be ready to play at the end of the skit a recording of the Celine Dion song "My Heart Will Go On" (from the soundtrack of the movie *Titanic*).

Other Options: If you have sufficient control over your lighting, light the **Elderly Rosie** and **Young Rosie** areas separately, turning on an area's lights only when a scene is being played there.

The Characters:
    Elderly Rosie, ancient but spunky
    Young Rosie, the woman **Elderly Rosie** used to be
    Zack, brash and arrogant young man
    Treasure Hunter, intense adventurer
    Assistant, male or female helper

*(As the skit begins, **Elderly Rosie**, **Treasure Hunter**, and **Assistant** sit in semicircle of chairs stage right. Two empty chairs sit stage left.)*

Hunter: *(Speaking loudly, as if Rosie might be deaf)* And SO, ROSIE, for YEARS we've been SEARCHING the OCEAN FLOOR to find where the SHIP went DOWN! Last WEEK, right HERE, we finally FOUND it!

Elderly Rosie: You don't have to SHOUT! I'm only 137 YEARS OLD, you know! It's not like I'm 138!

Hunter: Oh. RIGHT. Well, LAST WEEK we FINALLY found the WRECK.

Assistant: *(Showing **Elderly Rosie** two sheets from a sketch pad)* We ALSO found these PICTURES. ONE of them shows YOU wearing this BEAUTIFUL NECKLACE.

Hunter: We've GOT to find that NECKLACE!

Elderly Rosie: AH, yes. The NECKLACE! ZACK gave it to me, you know.

Hunter: ZACK?

Elderly Rosie: YES. Do you want to hear the WHOLE STORY?

Hunter: Well, SURE…if it won't take too LONG. After ALL, you ARE 138 YEARS OLD.

Elderly Rosie: 137!

Hunter: Oh. RIGHT.

Elderly Rosie: Let me tell you how I MET Zack. It was on the PROW of the SHIP. I REMEMBER it as if it were YESTERDAY…

*(They freeze. At the other side of the stage **Zack** enters, climbs onto a chair, and spreads his arms wide as if enjoying the feel of the wind against him. He maintains this pose throughout the scene. **Young Rosie** enters and runs up to him.)*

Young Rosie: SIR! Are you…trying to KILL yourself?

Zack: KILL myself? Are you KIDDING?

Young Rosie: But it's DANGEROUS to stand up there! You could FALL IN and DROWN!

Zack: HA! Not ME, baby! I'm…UNSINKABLE!

Young Rosie: REALLY, sir, you should be more CAREFUL.

Zack: FORGET it, baby! I'm gonna live FOREVER!

Young Rosie: But…NOBODY lives FOREVER, sir. SURELY you've heard…

Zack: And STOP calling me "SIR"! The name's ZACK!

Young Rosie: I SEE. TELL me about yourself, Zack. What is your OCCUPATION?

Zack: *(Shouting ecstatically into the "wind")* I'm…the KING OF THE WORLD!

Young Rosie: *(Awestruck)* REALLY?

*(**Zack** and **Young Rosie** freeze; the others "thaw.")*

Elderly Rosie: YES, I could tell right AWAY there was something DIFFERENT about Zack. I'd seen the KING OF NORWAY once, on a SARDINE CAN. But I'd never met…the KING of the WORLD.

Hunter: And is THAT when he gave you the NECKLACE?

Elderly Rosie: NO, no. That happened a few nights LATER. I remember it as if it were…the day BEFORE yesterday…

*(They freeze. At the other side of the stage, **Young Rosie** sits and poses while **Zack** draws on a large pad of paper he's holding.)*

Young Rosie: Oh, ZACK…you're such a GREAT ARTIST.

Zack: You got THAT right, baby!

Young Rosie: I can hardly WAIT to see this PORTRAIT.

Zack: It's a DOOZY, baby…a TRIBUTE to the most BEAUTIFUL person on this SHIP…the person I MOST ADORE!

Young Rosie: Oh, Zack, that's so SWEET. *(He hands her the pad; she looks at it.)* WAIT a minute! This is a picture of YOU!

Zack: You GOT it, baby! Because I'm…*(he stands on his chair, spreads his arms wide, and shouts ecstatically)* the KING OF THE WORLD!

Young Rosie: But, ZACK…don't you ever WONDER whether there might be a HIGHER POWER?

Zack: Higher than ME? THAT'S a good one! *(He takes necklace out of his pocket.)* Oh, by the WAY…put THIS on. *(He tosses necklace to her.)*

Young Rosie: What a LOVELY NECKLACE!

Zack: YEAH. I…uh…didn't STEAL it or ANYTHING.

Young Rosie: *(Putting on necklace)* And you want me to WEAR it while you draw my PICTURE, as a TOKEN of your LOVE.

Zack: NO, I want you to wear it so I can draw a picture of IT! YOU'LL be in there somewhere, TOO, I GUESS. *(He sits and picks up pad.)*

Young Rosie: Oh, ZACK…you ALWAYS know the RIGHT THING to SAY.

(They freeze. Others "thaw.")

Elderly Rosie: MY, that Zack had a WAY about him. I DREAMED about him every NIGHT. But then my dreams took a FRIGHTENING TURN. I remember it as if it were the day TWO WEEKS before LAST TUESDAY...

*(They freeze. Across the stage, **Zack** and **Young Rosie** "thaw." **Zack** climbs atop chair and spreads his arms against the "wind.")*

Young Rosie: Zack, I've been having BAD DREAMS...PREMONITIONS.

Zack: PREMONITIONS? About WHAT?

Young Rosie: I keep dreaming that something TERRIBLE is going to happen! A DISASTER! And that it's going to involve...an ICEBERG!

Zack: An ICEBERG? Baby, we're a MILLION MILES from the nearest ICEBERG. NOTHING'S going to happen to US. At least not to ME!

Young Rosie: But don't you think that just in case you DON'T live forever, you should be PREPARED?

Zack: No NEED, baby! Because I'm...the KING...of the UNIVERSE!

Young Rosie: You...you ARE?

Zack: I got PROMOTED!

(They freeze. Others "thaw.")

Elderly Rosie: The NEXT night...it HAPPENED.

Hunter: That's when...the SHIP went down?

Elderly Rosie: NO, no. We were at DINNER, Zack and I, with a group of RICH PEOPLE. ZACK was eating his SALAD, telling everyone he was the KING of the UNIVERSE, when he suddenly CHOKED on a piece of LETTUCE.

Assistant: LETTUCE? What KIND?

Elderly Rosie: ICEBERG.

Hunter: And did he...?

Elderly Rosie: YES. The HEIMLICH MANEUVER hadn't been INVENTED yet.

Hunter: And the SHIP?

Elderly Rosie: It went DOWN a few nights LATER. But EVERYBODY knows THAT story.

Hunter: And the NECKLACE? What happened to the NECKLACE?

Elderly Rosie: Oh, THAT old thing? I think it's in my PURSE. *(She finds it in her purse.)* You can HAVE it if you WANT. *(She gives it to **Treasure Hunter**.)* It's worth about A DOLLAR NINETY-NINE.

Hunter: WHAT? I've spent SIX YEARS and TEN MILLION DOLLARS to find a TWO-DOLLAR NECKLACE? I think…I'm going to THROW myself OVERBOARD! *(Dazed and staggering, he exits.)*

Assistant: *(Standing up, as does **Elderly Rosie**)* WELL, Rosie, you must MISS Zack…so BRASH, so DASHING, so HEADSTRONG.

Elderly Rosie: Are you NUTS? He was a JERK!

Assistant: YEAH, but…he was ONE of a KIND.

Elderly Rosie: I WISH!

*(**All** exit as the theme from the movie Titanic, Celine Dion's "My Heart Will Go On," plays over the sound system and finally fades out.)*

▶ **Related Scriptures:**
- Psalm 2
- Proverbs 16:5, 18-19
- James 4:13-17

▶ **Related Topics:**
- Preparing for Eternity
- Humility
- The brevity of life

Punched by an Angel

Topic: The Supernatural

The Scene: A deserted street

The Simple Setup: No set is needed. You'll need to make a set of wings for **Gabriel.** (White cardboard with drawn-in "feathers" will work.) Attach the wings using Velcro fasteners or straps around the actor's shoulders. **Winona** will need a binder with papers in it (her "script"). **Quinton** and **Winona** should wear "hip" clothes; **Gabriel** could wear either casual clothes or a white robe with his wings.

The Sound: If you're using stationary microphones, place one or two stage right and one or two stage left; plan the actors' movements accordingly.

Other Options: If you have time, you can make more realistic-looking wings for Gabriel by gluing cotton batting to the cardboard. Dressing him in a white suit would be a nice touch too.

The Characters:

    Gabriel, a strapping but polite angel with a pair of wings on his back

    Quinton Tarantula, volatile movie director

    Winona, the director's nervous assistant

*(As the skit begins, **Gabriel** is standing at the side of the stage as if waiting patiently for something. **Quinton** enters from opposite side, not noticing **Gabriel**, forming a "frame" with his hands and squinting through it as if through a camera lens, taking in everything except **Gabriel**.)*

Quinton: *(Looking around through his "frame")* Uh-huh. Uh-huh. YES! YES! It's PERFECT!

Winona: *(Rushing in breathlessly)* Did you…did you FIND something, sir?

Quinton: THIS is the PLACE! THIS is the street where I want to film SCENE 47! It's got just the right amount of GRIT, the right amount of GRIME for a QUINTON TARANTULA PICTURE!

Winona: Oh, YES, sir!

Quinton: We'll put the FOG MACHINE over THERE and the EXPLODING BABY CARRIAGES over THERE and…*(suddenly spotting **Gabriel**)* HEY! What have we got HERE? *(To **Winona**)* It's…it's an ANGEL!

Winona: Well, he DOES have those WINGS, sir.

Quinton: This guy is PERFECT! He's just what I NEED! What are the odds that we'd find him HERE? *(To Gabriel)* Hey, YOU!

Gabriel: Who, ME?

Quinton: How would you like to be a STAR?

Gabriel: Oh, I don't...

Quinton: I'm QUINTON TARANTULA. Maybe you've seen my FILMS...*RESERVOIR RATS...BEATEN TO A PULP WITH FRICTION...*

Gabriel: I've...HEARD of them, YES.

Quinton: And this is my ASSISTANT, RAMONA.

Winona: That's WINONA, sir.

Quinton: RIGHT. *(To Gabriel)* And YOU are?

Gabriel: You can call me...GABRIEL.

Quinton: OKAY, Gabe...here's the DEAL. My NEXT PICTURE is a real EPIC. VERY SPIRITUAL ...but with plenty of ACTION! I call it... *(raises hands and looks into the distance as if envisioning movie marquee)* PUNCHED BY AN ANGEL!

Gabriel: *PUNCHED BY AN ANGEL?*

Quinton: SURE! ANGELS are BIG! Look at that TRAVOLTA thing a while back...an angel who SMOKES, DRINKS, and SCRATCHES HIMSELF! DYNAMITE! You throw in a little JACKIE CHAN, you've got *PUNCHED BY AN ANGEL!*

Gabriel: I SEE.

Quinton: So I need a CELESTIAL BEING. Are YOU a celestial being, Gabe?

Gabriel: As a matter of fact, I AM.

Quinton: I KNEW it! Now, the part calls for you to do...well, typical ANGEL stuff. Like, uh... *(He snaps his fingers repeatedly at **Winona**.)*

Winona: *(Hurriedly consulting script)* Like...uh... *(Reading)* GIVING UP YOUR ANGELIC STATUS so you can discover how WONDERFUL it is to EAT CHOCOLATE and MAKE OUT.

Gabriel: We…don't DO that.

Winona: (Reading) And USING YOUR POWERS to help a LOSING BASEBALL TEAM win the CHAMPIONSHIP.

Gabriel: We don't do THAT, either.

Winona: (Reading) And GETTING EVEN with IRRITATING CHARACTERS by SMITING them with EARTHQUAKES and PESTILENCE.

Gabriel: We don't do that, EITHER…USUALLY.

Quinton: Now, JUST a MINUTE! Are you saying we don't know our ANGEL STUFF? I'll have you KNOW, pal, that we did TWO DAYS of EXTENSIVE RESEARCH! We watched EVERY show about angels that Hollywood ever MADE!

Gabriel: But did you…read the BIBLE?

Quinton: The BIBLE? Oh, you mean VARIETY?

Gabriel: NO. But NEVER MIND.

Quinton: FORGET it, Mr. Hotshot Angel. We'll make this picture WITH or WITHOUT you!

Gabriel: I wouldn't DO that if I were you.

Quinton: Oh, YEAH? Why NOT?

Gabriel: Because my…EMPLOYER was hoping I could CONVINCE you OTHERWISE. He feels there have been ENOUGH MISINFORMED PRODUCTIONS about the SUPERNATURAL.

Quinton: Is that RIGHT? Well, NOBODY tells QUINTON TARANTULA what pictures to make!

Gabriel: (Shrugging) Very WELL. (He waves his hand slowly in front of **Quinton**.)

Quinton: (Putting his hands to his face) AAGGHH! I can't SEE! I'm BLIND!

Gabriel: DON'T worry. It'll WEAR OFF…as soon as you SEE the LIGHT.

Quinton: RAMONA! Get me OUT of here! (**Winona** takes his arm and starts to lead him away.) You'll hear from my LAWYERS, FEATHER BOY! You can't DO this to QUINTON

TARANTULA! *(Winona "accidentally" leads him into the wall.)* OW! RAMONA, what are you DOING?

Winona: It's WINONA, sir. *(She smiles at **Gabriel** and exits with **Quinton**.)*

Gabriel: *(After a pause, to audience)* We don't really DO that... USUALLY. *(He exits.)*

▶ **Related Scriptures:**
- Psalm 91:9-16
- Hebrews 1
- Revelation 14:6–15:6

▶ **Related Topics:**
- Angels
- The authority of Scripture
- Hollywood and religion

A Show About Nothing

Topic: Priorities

The Scene: An apartment

The Simple Setup: For this spoof of the TV show *Seinfeld*, you can make the "apartment" as basic or as elaborate as you like. The simplest setup is to use a sofa. You'll need a portable phone or cell phone for **Jerky**. (It doesn't have to work.) Using actors who can physically and vocally resemble their *Seinfeld* counterparts will add depth to the skit. **New-Man** may look like his *Seinfeld* ancestor, but should be friendly rather than brooding. All can wear casual clothes, but **Jerky** and **Lame** should be dressed somewhat neatly and stylishly. If possible, give **Blamer** a loud, dated-looking shirt, and brush his hair so that it stands on end.

The Sound: If you're using stationary microphones, place one by the door, one in front of the sofa, and one or two more beside the sofa, depending on where **Jerky** and **Lame** will do most of their standing.

Other Options: For extra fun, try playing some bass guitar riffs recorded from the transitional music of a *Seinfeld* rerun at the beginning and end of your skit.

The Characters:

> **Jerky Steinfeld**, a man obsessed with the trivial
> **Gorge**, his similarly obsessed male friend
> **Lame**, their similarly obsessed female friend
> **Blamer**, their strange and similarly obsessed male friend
> **New-Man**, their former friend, no longer similarly obsessed

*(As the skit begins, **Jerky** stands in his apartment, answering the phone.)*

Jerky: HELLO? Yes, this is JERKY STEINFELD. You're with WHO? The CANCER SOCIETY? Didja EVER NOTICE how NEGATIVE that word "CANCER" sounds? I mean, it's not just a DISEASE, it's also a CONSTELLATION…CANCER the CRAB. And who likes a CRAB? I mean, they're okay to EAT if you've got some of that HORSE-RADISH SAUCE, but… *(Pauses.)* HELLO? *(Puts phone down.)* WELL! SHE was kind of…CRABBY. *(**Gorge** enters.)* Oh, it's YOU, Gorge.

Gorge: YEAH, Jerky, it's ME. *(Sits.)* Didja EVER NOTICE how many CRACKS there are in the SIDEWALK between YANKEE STADIUM and HERE? There are exactly 938.

Jerky: How do you KNOW?

Gorge: I just COUNTED 'em. TWICE.

Jerky: And you got the same number BOTH TIMES?

Gorge: Well, NO. Once I got 937 and once 939. So I ADDED them and divided by TWO.

Jerky: Gorge, Gorge, GORGE! That's an AVERAGE! That's not ACCURATE!

Gorge: You're RIGHT. I'll go back and count again TOMORROW. I'll KEEP counting until I come up with the SAME NUMBER at least 12 TIMES!

Jerky: THAT'S the spirit! *(Lame enters.)* Oh, HI, Lame.

Lame: HI, Jerky. HI, Gorge. *(To both of them)* Didja EVER NOTICE that the ELEVATOR BUTTON for this floor has some kind of GUNK on it?

Gorge: You mean that GRAY gunk, about a SIXTEENTH OF AN INCH from the TOP, approximately 20 DEGREES to the LEFT of PERPENDICULAR?

Jerky: No, that's the "CLOSE DOOR" button. She's talking about the BROWNISH gunk directly under the NUMERAL and shaped like a CRESCENT MOON.

Lame: RIGHT! Except it's shaped more like a FINGERNAIL CLIPPING with a SLIGHTLY IRREGULAR CONVEX SURFACE.

Jerky: YEP, that's the ONE!

Gorge: Of COURSE! I REMEMBER it now!

Lame: Well, you'll have to HOLD ON to that memory, because…it's NOT THERE ANYMORE!

Jerky: WHAT?

Gorge: You're KIDDING!

Lame: I wish I WERE. I can't IMAGINE what HAPPENED!

Gorge: Probably some PUNK KID with a PAPER TOWEL and a bottle of FANTASTIK!

Jerky: This is TERRIBLE! It's like the whole WORLD has CHANGED! *(Enter Blamer, rushing in and stopping suddenly, looking disoriented.)* BLAMER!

Blamer: JERKY! LAME! GORGE! Did you…hear the NEWS?

Lame: You mean about the GUNK on the ELEVATOR BUTTON?

Blamer: That's RIGHT! Man, this is…APOCALYPTIC! I haven't been this UPSET since…since the NEW YORK TIMES accidentally put a "6" at the top of page 5! *(Shivering uncontrollably)* OOHH!

(There is a knock at the door.)

Jerky: WHAT? Somebody around here KNOCKS? *(To person at door)* It's OPEN!

*(**New-Man** enters, smiling politely.)*

Jerky: Oh, it's YOU, NEW-MAN.

Lame: *(To Gorge)* Now that he's become a NEW-MAN, he gives me the CREEPS!

Gorge: *(To Lame)* Me, TOO!

New-Man: *(Enthusiastically addressing the rest)* Didja EVER NOTICE how BEAUTIFUL the SUNSET is?

Others: *(Unison)* WHAT?

New-Man: Didja EVER NOTICE how many NEEDY PEOPLE there are around us who could USE our HELP?

Others: *(Unison)* HUH?

New-Man: Didja EVER NOTICE how SHORT life is…and that we need to LIFT OUR EYES above TRIVIAL things so that we don't miss what's truly IMPORTANT?

Others: *(Unison)* WHAT?!?

New-Man: Well, just thought I'd DROP BY. See you all LATER! *(He exits.)*

Blamer: *(After a pause)* He—he's RIGHT, you know.

Lame: All we ever THINK about is MEANINGLESS TRIVIA.

Gorge: All we ever TALK about are TINY DETAILS of ABSOLUTELY NO SIGNIFICANCE.

Jerky: Our LIVES are about…NOTHING!

Lame: NADA!

Gorge: ZIP!

Blamer:		We—we could CHANGE. We could FORGET about all those NITPICKY LITTLE THINGS.
Gorge:		We could focus on what's IMPORTANT!
Lame:		We could get our PRIORITIES straight!
Jerky:		Our lives could actually be about...SOMETHING!

(They all stop and look at each other.)

All:		*(Unison, after pause)* NAH!!!
Gorge:		Let's go to the COFFEE SHOP.
Lame:		We can look at that ELEVATOR BUTTON on the way!

(They start to exit.)

Blamer:		Maybe that PUNK KID with the PAPER TOWEL meant to clean the "CLOSE DOOR" button INSTEAD!
Jerky:		*(As **All** exit)* Didja EVER NOTICE how the MOLECULAR STRUCTURE of PAPER TOWEL FIBERS is SIMILAR to that of FACIAL TISSUE? I mean, what's up with THAT?

▶ **Related Scriptures:**
- Ecclesiastes 2:1-11
- Colossians 2:8
- Titus 3:8-9

▶ **Related Topics:**
- Putting God's kingdom first
- Redeeming the time
- Finding meaning in life

The Slide Show

Topic: Missions

The Scene: A living room

The Simple Setup: You'll need two chairs, a small table, a telephone stand, and a slide projector. (Be sure you have a place to plug it in.) Props include two slide carousels, a telephone, a large roll of duct tape, and a cookie. Put the slide projector on the table, pointing it offstage. (There's no need to put slides in the carousels, but the light in the projector should work.) Put the telephone on the stand, and place the stand near **Goforth**'s chair. The door for **Goforth**'s entrance can be real or imaginary; the entrance used by **Man in White Coat** should be out of sight of the audience. Costume for **Hypermeyer** should be "traditional housewife," perhaps including an apron. **Goforth**'s clothes should be neat but not terribly stylish. **Man in White Coat** should look like a hospital aide. At the end of the skit, after the lights go out, you may want to have **Offstage Policeman** and **Man in White Coat** carry out the chair-bound **Goforth**.

The Sound: If you're using stationary microphones, put one offstage, one near each of the chairs, and one next to the phone. Knocking can be done offstage; the door-breaking crash can be made by dropping a large piece of plywood on the floor.

Other Options: A love seat or overstuffed chair will further identify the living room.

The Characters:
>   **Helen Hypermeyer**, housewife on the edge
>   **Becky Goforth**, visiting missionary
>   **Offstage Policeman**
>   **Man in White Coat**

*(As the skit begins, **Hypermeyer** bustles about the living room, dusting and humming happily. Knocking sound. **Hypermeyer** goes to the door and opens it.)*

Goforth:	😊	Mrs. HYPERMEYER? I'm Becky GOFORTH.
Hypermeyer:	😊	The VISITING MISSIONARY! Please come IN! *(Pauses.)* I see you've brought your SLIDES.
Goforth:	😊	Of COURSE! What would a VISITING MISSIONARY be without SLIDES? *(She laughs. **Hypermeyer** joins in politely.)*
Hypermeyer:	😊	Here's the SLIDE PROJECTOR. And there's a SCREEN over THERE. *(Points offstage, same direction in which projector is aimed.)*
Goforth:	😊	GREAT! *(Sets her slide carousel by projector.)* And will… your HUSBAND be joining us?

Hypermeyer: He's...uh...OUT of TOWN.

Goforth: Oh. *(Looks around.)* And the OTHERS you invited, are THEY on their way?

Hypermeyer: Um...YES! I'm sure they MUST be. Won't you sit DOWN?

Goforth: THANK you. *(She sits in chair.)*

Hypermeyer: Would you like some COFFEE?

Goforth: Oh, NO, thank you.

Hypermeyer: TEA?

Goforth: NO, thanks.

Hypermeyer: COOKIE?

Goforth: NO, no, I'm FINE.

Hypermeyer: Then how about some— DUCT TAPE? *(She yanks a big roll of duct tape from behind the slide projector and feverishly starts wrapping tape around **Goforth** and the chair, trapping her.)*

Goforth: DUCT TAPE? What are you—I don't UNDERSTAND!

Hypermeyer: *(Continuing to wrap despite **Goforth**'s struggles)* Oh, YOU will! YOU will!

Goforth: It's like you're TYING ME UP! I can't get out of the CHAIR!

Hypermeyer: That's the IDEA, sister! *(She finishes taping, then stands back to survey her handiwork, huffing and puffing.)*

Goforth: *(After a pause)* Those PEOPLE you said you INVITED...they're not COMING, ARE they?

Hypermeyer: RIGHT.

Goforth: And there's not going to be a SLIDE SHOW, is there?

Hypermeyer: Of COURSE there is! *(She takes another slide carousel from behind the projector and loads it as she talks in an increasing frenzy.)* Just not the one you EXPECTED...not the MISSIONARY slide show...not the one where you show a little NATIVE man who used to have 700 WIVES and now he HELPS you by WALKING OVER 50 MILES OF BROKEN GLASS EVERY DAY so he can PREACH in the next VILLAGE! Not THAT slide show! *(She sits and switches on the projector, which shines in the direction of the imaginary, offstage screen.)* No, THIS time you have to watch MY pictures! THEN you'll see! THEN you'll know what it's like! *(She pauses, composes herself, and speaks sweetly.)* Are you SURE you wouldn't like some TEA?

Goforth: Uh…I don't think I could hold the CUP right now.

Hypermeyer: Oh. Of COURSE. *(She turns back to the projector.)* Now, where WERE we? *(She pushes the projector button to change the slide.)* AH, yes. This is ENRIQUE, who bags my GROCERIES down at the SUPERMARKET. I spend a LOT OF MONEY at the supermarket. It takes a LOT OF EXPENSIVE FOOD to feed a HUSBAND and TWO TEENAGERS. *(Suddenly ranting, out of control)* So is it any WONDER that I didn't put any MONEY in the SPECIAL MISSIONS OFFERING THREE WEEKS AGO? IS it? Well, IS it?

Goforth: I…GUESS not.

Hypermeyer: *(Sweetly)* Very GOOD. *(She pushes the projector button.)* THIS is our CAR. I spend a LOT OF TIME in our car…ERRANDS to run, SCHOOL FUNCTIONS and CHURCH MEETINGS to attend, KIDS to shuttle to the MALL and KARATE LESSONS and their FRIENDS' HOUSES! *(Suddenly ranting, out of control)* So is it any WONDER that I don't have TIME to read all those PRAYER LETTERS from our church's MISSIONARIES that they put on that TABLE in the FOYER every month? Well, IS it? IS it?

Goforth: N-no.

Hypermeyer: *(Sweetly)* EXACTLY! NOW, are you SURE you wouldn't like one of those COOKIES? They're PECAN SANDIES, with just a TOUCH of POWDERED SUGAR!

Goforth: *(Looking around)* O-OK.

Hypermeyer: I'll be RIGHT BACK.

*(**Hypermeyer** exits. **Goforth**, as quickly as she can, scoots her chair over to the telephone. She removes the receiver with her teeth and puts it on the telephone stand. She pushes three of the touch-tone buttons with her nose, then talks into the mouthpiece.)*

Goforth: Hello, 911? I'm at 4234 MAPLEWOOD LANE. I'm being held PRISONER by a CRAZY WOMAN! *(She glances in the direction of **Hypermeyer**'s exit, then scoots her chair back to where it was. She tries to smile as **Hypermeyer** enters with a cookie.)*

Hypermeyer: HERE we go! Hope you LIKE it! *(She sticks the cookie between **Goforth's** teeth. **Goforth** holds it there for the rest of the skit.)* Let's SEE… *(**Hypermeyer** sits and pushes projector button.)* Oh, YES. THIS is a plateful of our TYPICAL NATIVE FOODS. There's a HAMBURGER, and some CHIPS, and some RASPBERRY GELATIN, with a GLASS of DIET COLA. SOMETIMES, on SPECIAL OCCASIONS, we have an EXOTIC DELICACY called HOSTESS TWINKIES. THESE are the kinds of foods we've ALWAYS EATEN. *(Suddenly ranting, out of control)* So is it any WONDER that I can't POSSIBLY become a MISSIONARY and move to some AWFUL FOREIGN COUNTRY where they eat BUGS and SHEEP'S EYES? Well, IS it? IS it?

Goforth: *(With cookie still in her mouth)* MWFF! MMFLF!

Hypermeyer: I KNOW what you're SAYING…that you're BETTER than I am! *(**Goforth** shakes head. **Hypermeyer** stands and moves menacingly toward **Goforth**.)* Well, you can't make me feel GUILTY anymore, Missy MISSIONARY! I'll see to it that you NEVER make ANYONE feel guilty AGAIN!

(Loud, long knocking sounds.)

Hypermeyer: *(Sweetly)* Well, now, who could THAT be?

Offstage Policeman: Open UP! POLICE!

Hypermeyer: *(To **Goforth**)* YOU! YOU called them!

Offstage Policeman: BREAK DOWN THE DOOR! *(Crashing sound)* FREEZE, lady! *(**Hypermeyer** slumps, looking surly.)* OKAY, Fred! She's all YOURS!

*(**Man in White Coat** enters and takes **Hypermeyer** by the arm.)*

Man in White Coat: ALL right, ma'am. Time to come with ME. We have a NICE, FLUFFY CELL waiting for you.

Hypermeyer: *(Being led away)* But SHE'S the one! Don't you SEE? Making us all feel GUILTY with her SELF-SACRIFICE and her OUTDATED SHOES and her KNOWING THE NAMES OF COUNTRIES THE REST OF US NEVER HEARD OF! SHE'S the one!

*(**Hypermeyer** exits with **Man in White Coat**. After a pause, **Goforth** drops the cookie from her teeth.)*

Goforth: *(To herself)* Is it too late to become...a plumber? *(The lights go out.)*

▶ **Related Scriptures:**
- Matthew 28:16-20
- Luke 10:38-42
- John 4:34-38

▶ **Related Topics:**
- Guilt
- Evangelism
- Expectations

The Y-Files

Topic: Suffering

The Scene: A dark, abandoned warehouse

The Simple Setup: This is a spoof of the TV show, *The X-Files*. The stage should be dark enough for the flashlight beams to show, but not so dark that the audience can't see what the actors are doing. You'll need a fairly high bookcase or a shelf with an open, unmarked sack on it. The sack should contain at least a dozen toy rubber insects, the bigger the better. Give **Moldy** and **Sculler** flashlights; have them wear suits. Use an offstage flash camera or strobe for the flash during the explosion. Sculler will need a cell phone that will ring during the skit.

The Sound: If you're using stationary microphones, place one offstage and two or three spaced evenly across the stage. Plan the movements of **Moldy** and **Sculler** so that they can deliver their lines at the onstage mikes. You may want to add a low mike at the spot where **Sculler** will kneel and **Moldy** will search for his pin. You'll also need a recorded "explosion" sound effect and spooky music from The *X-Files* TV show, or something similar. The spooky theme music is optional but will add depth to the skit.

Other Options: A dim blue light trained on the stage will add to the spooky effect.

The Characters:

        Announcer, ominous-sounding

        Agent Moldy, paranoid, male FBI investigator

        Agent Sculler, skeptical, female FBI investigator

(As the skit begins, the stage is empty.)

Announcer: *(Offstage, through sound system)* NEXT on FLOX —*THE Y-FILES.*

(Sound of spooky music.)

*(Enter **Moldy** and **Sculler** from opposite sides, searching in the dark with flashlights, not seeing each other. Music fades out.)*

Sculler: MOLDY? AGENT MOLDY? Are you THERE?

Moldy: SCULLER? SCULLER, is that YOU?

Sculler: It's so hard to SEE in this ABANDONED WAREHOUSE! Why can't we ever investigate things with the LIGHTS ON?

Moldy: Watch your STEP, Sculler. You never KNOW what might be lurking in the…

*(Suddenly **Sculler** trips and falls.)*

Sculler: OW! I TRIPPED over a LOOSE BOARD! My NYLONS are in SHREDS! Oh, Moldy... WHY do things like this have to HAPPEN? WHY?

Moldy: WHY, Sculler? The answer is CLEAR. The BOARD was LOOSENED by the TELEKINETIC POWERS of a MUTANT raised in a SECRET GOVERNMENT LABORATORY!

Sculler: OH. But how do you...

Moldy: No time for DETAILS! We've got to continue our INVESTIGATION. Just REMEMBER our MOTTO.

Sculler: What's THAT?

Moldy: TRUST NOBODY.

Sculler: How do I know that's REALLY our motto?

Moldy: TRUST me.

*(Flashlights pointed, they walk cautiously in opposite directions. **Sculler** bumps into a wall and feels it with her hand. She finds a shelf with an open sack on it.)*

Sculler: What's THIS? A SACK? What do you suppose is in...

(She takes the sack off the shelf and turns it upside down over her uplifted face as if to look into it. Out comes a load of real-looking rubber insects.)

Sculler: *(Sputtering and frantically brushing things out of her hair)* AAUGGHH! BUGS! Oh, they're HORRIBLE! *(She stamps on them.)* MOLDY! WHY do things like THIS have to happen? WHY? WHY?

Moldy: WHY, Sculler? Obviously a UFO was attempting to ABDUCT you, and the SACK was meant as BAIT. But the ALIEN TRACTOR BEAM was NEUTRALIZED by the HIDDEN DEPOSITS of MARTIAN OOZE buried here THOUSANDS OF YEARS AGO. If NOT, you'd be the subject of HIDEOUS EXPERIMENTS by now. You should be GRATEFUL.

Sculler: REALLY? Well, HOW do you explain...

Moldy: No TIME! Back to our INVESTIGATION. And try to be more CAREFUL.

*(Flashlights pointed, they start looking around again. Just then **Sculler's** cell phone rings.)*

Sculler: Agent Sculler. WHAT? NO! THAT CAN'T BE! *(Dazed, she puts the phone away.)*

Moldy: What is it NOW?

Sculler: I just LOST EVERYTHING in the STOCK MARKET! I'm RUINED! WHY do things like THIS have to happen? WHY? WHY?

Moldy: WHY, Sculler? It's SIMPLE. A SHADOW GOVERNMENT consisting of the INTER-NATIONAL MONETARY FUND and the NATIONAL MODEL RAILROADING ASSOCIATION has MANIPULATED GLOBAL MARKETS BEHIND THE SCENES to produce a TRADING DOWNTURN resulting in the ECONOMIC DESTABILIZATION of EVERYONE WHOSE FIRST NAME STARTS WITH "S."

Sculler: I don't see how…*(Pauses.)* WAIT! I HAVEN'T lost everything! I still have some CASH and JEWELRY in my PURSE! It's over THERE, in my CAR! *(She points stage right.)*

(From stage right there is a flash of light and sound of explosion.)

Sculler: My CAR! My CAR just BLEW UP! *(She falls to her knees.)* WHY? WHY DO THINGS LIKE THIS HAPPEN?

Moldy: WHY, Sculler? ANYONE can see that the MAJOR AUTO MANUFACTURERS, working in concert with a RACE OF EXTRATERRESTRIAL CATERPILLARS, decided to…

Sculler: *(Standing)* SHUT UP! Just SHUT UP! You're driving me CRAZY with your STUPID CONSPIRACY THEORIES! *(She starts choking him.)*

Moldy: STOP! You don't know what you're DOING! You might loosen my…*(He feels his lapel.)* My PIN! My FBI pin! You made it fall OFF! *(Sculler lets him go.)* My PIN! How am I ever going to FIND it? *(He goes to his hands and knees and searches the floor.)* Oh, WHY do things like this HAPPEN? WHY? WHY?

Sculler: WHY, Moldy? Because you're an IDIOT…and because I have a BAD TEMPER!

Moldy: That's RIDICULOUS! It's GOT to be a CONSPIRACY! A CONSPIRACY, I tell you! *(Wailing, he searches in vain for his pin.)*

Sculler: WELL, Moldy…I'm not sure why there's SUFFERING in the world. I guess we'll just go on searching NEXT week.

Moldy: My precious PIN! Oh, where's CIGARETTE CHOMPING MAN when I need him? Where are the BONEHEADED GUNMEN?

Sculler: See you NEXT week, Moldy. Until then, REMEMBER our OTHER motto.

Moldy: What's THAT?

Sculler: The TRUTH… *(pointing flashlight up)* is UP there. *(She shines light on herself and puts hand on her heart.)* And maybe in HERE, too.

*(She exits, leaving **Moldy** to search the floor and sob as the stage goes dark. Sound: spooky theme music up and out.)*

▶ **Related Scriptures:**
- Genesis 3:17-19
- Job 5:6-7
- Romans 8:18-39

▶ **Related Topics:**
- God's sovereignty
- Comforting others
- Tough questions

Scripture Index

Topical Index

Group Publishing, Inc.
Attention: Product Development
P.O. Box 481
Loveland, CO 80539
Fax: (970) 679-4370

Evaluation for *High-Impact Worship Dramas*

Please help Group Publishing, Inc., continue to provide innovative and useful resources for ministry. Please take a moment to fill out this evaluation and mail or fax it to us. Thanks!

● ● ●

1. As a whole, this book has been (circle one)

not very helpful   very helpful

1   2   3   4   5   6   7   8   9   10

2. The best things about this book:

3. Ways this book could be improved:

4. Things I will change because of this book:

5. Other books I'd like to see Group publish in the future:

6. Would you be interested in field-testing future Group products and giving us your feedback? If so, please fill in the information below:

Name _____

Street Address _____

City _____ State _____ Zip _____

Phone Number _____ Date _____